**OFFICE FOR STANDARDS
IN EDUCATION**

Artists
IN SCHOOLS

a review

DAVID ODDIE
Director of the Barefoot Project
and GARTH ALLEN
Director of the Centre for Social and Educational Research,

University College of St Mark and St John

London: The Stationery Office

Office for Standards in Education
Alexandra House
33 Kingsway
London WC2B 6SE
Internet: www.ofsted.gov.uk

First published 1998

ISBN 0 11 350103 X

CONTENTS

PREFACE

In January 1997 OFSTED held a conference to discuss *Setting the Scene* published the previous year by the then Department of National Heritage (DNH). 'Setting the Scene' focused on the arts and young people and OFSTED invited a group of artists to run a series of workshops with HMIs throughout the conference. The inspectors were stimulated to explore key issues and questions through active engagement with the practice itself. The encounter between practising artists and inspectors was lively and productive. As a practitioner it was encouraging to see senior OFSTED staff talking with real passion about their values and beliefs in education and the role of the arts within their vision.

During the course of the conference it became apparent that further information about the work of artists in schools across the country would be helpful. Such information could include background material, a snapshot picture of current practice, provision and problems and an indication of the benefits arising. The process would help to give inspectors a framework within which they could relate inputs from artists to their own inspection priorities. I was therefore delighted when Christine Agambar, the Head of Research and Analysis at OFSTED, asked me to undertake a review of the work of artists in schools to achieve this purpose.

I appreciated OFSTED's decision to ask a practitioner to lead the review. Nineteen years ago I left teaching in one school to work in theatre in education. I established a company in Plymouth which also manages a theatre building with a range of courses and activities in different art forms. More recently I had set up the Barefoot Project specifically to promote greater understanding of the work of artists in education.

To balance my practical experience in the field with academic rigour I invited Garth Allen, Director of the Centre for Social and Educational Research at the University College of St Mark and St John in Plymouth and a highly experienced researcher and writer, to collaborate with me. I took the responsibility for researching and collecting data, visiting projects, interviewing key people and writing draft papers. Garth was my 'research minder', constantly reading and helping to re-draft and structure the document as we went along. The tension between our respective disciplines reflected the relationship between artist and teacher that we were investigating.

The review complements *The Arts Inspected: Good Teaching in Art, Dance, Drama and Music,* (Heinemann, 1998) which is a review of good arts in education teaching written by OFSTED's Specialist Advisers for art, dance, drama and music.

We are deeply grateful for the consistent support of David Read, Research Manager at OFSTED, and for his invaluable patience and encouragement.

David Oddie

INTRODUCTION

Intention

OFSTED is primarily concerned with the improvement of standards in schools through the process of inspection. The authors of the review are therefore committed to further the beneficial impact on teaching and learning of artists working in schools. The intention is to provide a framework that will encourage a greater understanding of the values and possibilities of involving a wide range of artists in education. It is hoped that the review will be valuable to teachers, artists, arts organisations that are involved directly in schools, inspectors and advisers; and that an important outcome will be furthering and improving dialogue between the worlds of the arts and education.

Many teachers are artists in their own right and the dividing line between artist and teacher is not clear cut. For the purposes of the review, the term 'artist' is used to denote someone who is engaged in the daily, professional practice of their art and who enters into a contractual relationship with a school or college to deliver a service. The service may involve a presentation or it may be a workshop process; it may be a combination of both. The artist may work in a large arts organisation, such as a theatre or gallery, or work independently from home.

A great deal of valuable research has already been done on the issue of artists in schools. The review builds on this work and seeks to provide a picture of practice, from a practitioner's perspective; it looks at the roots and development of artists' work in schools and surveys the current situation. A summary of the claims made for working with artists is provided and the benefits, and problems, are illustrated with reference to a small number of projects in a range of art forms.

The focus of the review is on the creative working relationship between artist and teacher and it raises questions as to how this core relationship can be enhanced and developed.

Artists and inspection

It was important in the early stages of the project to discover how OFSTED inspectors wrote about the work of artists in school during the course of Section 10 inspections. We searched the OFSTED database for references to artists working in schools, covering a twelve month period. There were many passing references in praise of a project or visit, and some reflections on the lack of input from artists. The majority of references were in the section of the report covering Spiritual, Moral, Social and Cultural Development. The main categories of reference can be summarised as follows:

- general claims to enrichment
- encouragement of pupils as performers and composers

- stimulus for staff
- good example of community involvement
- enhancement of learning
- promotion of cultural development, understanding and diversity.

Inspectors saw the main benefit of such projects as the promotion of cultural development, understanding and diversity. It was apparent that one objective of the review would be to encourage a more active and detailed involvement of inspectors in the appraisal of artist in school projects. Such involvement would enhance recognition of the value of the work across the curriculum and help to raise standards.

Outline

Chapter 1: Historical Backgound

The review begins with a historical background which focuses on key developments and concepts. These include the idea of artists being resident in schools, the emergence of education officers and departments within arts organisations, the growth of dedicated arts in education companies and the activities of freelance artists who work in a range of community settings.

The background then examines how major events during the eighties and nineties, such as the Education Reform Act, affected these developments. The survey describes a range of initiatives that evolved to build up new structures and mechanisms of support for artists in education. Such initiatives included the creation of new funding partnerships with agencies such as health authorities, the introduction of the Lottery, commercial sponsorship and the appearance of specialist arts education agencies.

Chapter 2: A Survey of the Current Situation

Chapter 2 examines the current framework within which artists and teachers work together. The chapter looks at the educational activities of mainstream arts organisations funded by the Arts Council of England (ACE) and the Regional Arts Boards (RABs), and the current situation facing dedicated arts companies and freelance artists. The key concept of artists working within a range of partnerships is then explored in relation to local education authorities (LEAs), RABs and the continued development of arts education agencies. The chapter concludes with some observations on the training of both artists and teachers.

A survey of the experiences of artists and companies who work regularly in and with schools was undertaken in order to understand the current situation from their perspective. Two hundred artists were invited to provide a short testimony of the possibilities, problems and limitations they have experienced over recent years and to contribute their own views as to the educational significance and outcomes of their work. Over one hundred responses were received and these have been integrated into the main narrative.

Chapter 3: Summary of Claims

Over the course of the past four decades a number of claims have been made for benefits arising from the work of artists in schools. The claims have been made by practising artists, teachers, arts and education officers, academics and others. Chapter 3 summarises this wide range of claims and also provides a short survey of typical problems and tensions experienced by teachers and artists in the delivery of an artist(s)-in-school project.

The chapter relates the claims to the appropriate sections of the OFSTED *Framework for Inspection*. The claims are then supported by observations and comments illustrating the broad constituency of interests that acknowledge the significance of the work of artists in schools.

Chapter 4: The Practice

The benefits and problems arising from the work are illustrated with reference to seven contrasting artists-in-schools projects in a range of art forms. A series of interviews with participating artists, teachers, pupils and funders enabled and encouraged those involved to reflect upon the projects' impact and effectiveness. The interviews took place a considerable time after the completion of the projects.

We show how specific projects related, for example, to priorities and programmes of study within the National Curriculum. To encapsulate the living, felt experience of teachers and children, which in a good project may be inspirational, we have allowed those involved to speak for themselves.

Features which contributed to a successful outcome for the projects are summarised at the end of the chapter.

Selecting the projects

Given the limited time span at our disposal seven projects were chosen representing a wide range of work. Choosing seven projects out of the wealth of work taking place in schools demanded strict selection criteria:

- there should be a range of discrete art forms or a rich mix of art forms
- at least one of the artists should have significant experience of working in schools
- a range of schools should be represented
- the projects should cover a range of social and cultural contexts, for example, inner city, suburban and rural
- there should be a contrasting range of aims and objectives
- some of the schools should already have been inspected by OFSTED.

Interview framework for artists and schools

Artists, teachers and children involved were invited to tell the story of each project from beginning to end (Schechner, 1989:16-21). The following headings served as guidelines:

- **Genesis** – how the project originated

- **Planning** – how the whole process was structured, co-ordinated, planned and related to the curriculum

- **Organisation** – how the use of space, time, liaison between artist and school was negotiated

- **Preparation** – how the project was devised and developed; how students were prepared

- **Engagement** – how artist, teacher and students were involved in the delivery of the product or process

- **Follow-up** – whether there was any related or integrated follow-up activity

- **Evaluation** – how the project was evaluated and reflected upon by both artist and school.

Each stage was then the focus of further, more searching questions. These gave participants the opportunity to comment on aspects of their project that they thought worked well, as well as aspects that were less successful in their view, and to reflect on the effectiveness and impact of the project. The questions were devised so that the same questions would be put to both artist and teacher. Headteachers were interviewed to establish how such projects were considered within overall school policy, and how they were planned, budgeted for and evaluated.

The headings given to the individual projects are for reference purposes within the review and are not the original titles.

Chapter 5: Summary of Key Findings

Finally, a summary of key findings draws together observations and reflections from the projects and the other sections of the review.

1 HISTORICAL BACKGROUND

A bridge is being built without a blueprint. On the one side, there is the education pier, solid but, perhaps a little unimaginative. On the other is the arts pier, a much more eclectic construction, exhibiting a range of styles. Both sides have set out to construct a linking span but it is not yet clear whether the connection will be made. (Turner and Stronach, 1993: 39)

Early developments

The tradition of actors, musicians and other artists working in schools goes back a long way and practising artists have always influenced teachers of the arts. However, it is only in relatively recent times that the relationship has become more direct and formalised. Writers, dancers, musicians and visual artists-in-residence schemes and theatre in education programmes, for example, have all become features of the wider educational landscape.

'The State of the Arts'

A recent research project, 'The State of the Arts', (Ross and Kamba, 1997) carried out by the University of Exeter School of Education, asked teachers of the arts to prioritise major influences on their practice. Top of the list came 'visiting artists'. This may indeed reflect an affirmation and enhanced understanding of the positive benefits arising from working with artists. It may also, as we explore later, be a response to the changes arising from central government legislation during the past fifteen years to important local authority support services.

Artists work within a framework of educational, social and political structures, demands and expectations. How artists are used and invited into schools is a reflection of wider issues. For example, within the arts education world itself the debate between those seeking to promote an arts ethic grounded in a tradition, and those committed to progressive, 'child-centred' ideals, has continued to create much debate. The pendulum swings between those who prioritise the aims of aesthetic appreciation and those committed to the value of art as a vehicle for personal, social development and change.

The relationship of artists to schools reflects this debate. For example, writers-in-residence schemes initially focused on promoting an understanding of a writer's own work, then, with the development of a more 'child-centred' focus in educational thinking, the writer was used to stimulate children's own writing and thinking (Harries, 1983). The emphasis shifted from appreciation to active participation. In turn the focus on social issues and progressive ideas provoked a reaction leading to a keener interest in the actual skills, the craft of writing. A parallel process took place in other art forms (Taylor and Andrews, 1993: 37). This 'conservationist' perspective emphasised the need for children to be plugged into a sense of rich cultural tradition, an aesthetic field from which they could draw inspiration, ideas and skills (Abbs, 1987: 47).

As a result there is a huge diversity of artists-in-schools practice. Over the years a wide variety of ways in which artists engage with schools has evolved. Despite the dominance of specific forms at particular times, alternative models, which prioritise contrasting approaches and values, continue to exist. For example, in educational theatre the pendulum has swung from an emphasis on issue based work, predominant in the sixties and seventies, to activities that focus on the language and skills of theatre itself. However, issue based work continues to exist and some practitioners have developed sophisticated partnerships with agencies, such as health authorities, which would have been unthinkable twenty years ago.

Throughout the twentieth century, significant artists have also had a major influence on the development of arts in education philosophies and approaches. The impact of Rudolf Laban and Jacques Dalcroze on dance education, the training techniques and approaches of Kodaly and Carl Orff in music, illustrate the essential dynamic between arts education and the living world of the arts.

It is self-evident that artists working in different art forms may make varying demands on a school in terms of the use of space and resources. For example, a resident writer may find it easier than a dancer to work in a classroom. However, in looking at the history of artists in schools in relation to their discrete art forms there appear to be a number of common threads and developments. These developments are summarised below and are drawn on later to inform our examination of current practice.

The residency

The Gulbenkian Foundation initiated an artists-in-residence scheme in 1973 which raised key questions about the problems to be addressed within the artist/school relationship. The intention of the scheme was to involve artists, children, teachers and the local authority in a creative partnership that would open up new thinking about the relationship of artists to society. The Foundation hoped that each scheme would:

- 'place the artist in a new relationship to society, in an economically secure framework, to encourage a new sense of commitment and purpose; to give new material

- give children an insight into the creative processes at work, a broader appreciation of art and the artists (without formally teaching the children); to demythologise art for them

- encourage local authorities and teachers to depart from examination syllabuses and take a broader humanistic view of education' (Braden, 1978: 65).

The Arts Council sought to develop this concept in 1976 and immediately involved the Regional Arts Associations in organising the residencies.

For example, the idea of writers working directly in schools arose from the Literature Panel of the Arts Council of Great Britain (ACGB) in 1967. (The Arts Council did not appoint its own Education Officer until 1980.) The initial schemes involved writers visiting schools to read from and talk about their own work. Most of the work took place around London. By the late seventies the Regional Arts Associations (RAAs) were seeking a wider regional involvement and writers were also becoming more actively involved in workshop processes.

In the later eighties Eastern Arts encouraged a more organic approach with writers. This involved a series of readings and mini residencies providing the opportunity for a writer and children to work together more systematically. The idea of the workshop structure which emphasised process rather than product paralleled developments in other art forms.

By the later eighties there was a growing wealth of diverse experiences and approaches, ranging from the one-off visit to the longer-term residency. The residency seemed to be most effective when the artist was clearly seen and understood to be working as a practising artist, for example, when a visual artist set up a studio in the school. The process was less effective when the artist was perceived as an extra supply teacher. The support structure provided by the LEA subject adviser was also seen as a significant contributing feature for success (Braden 1978: 79). Despite the increasingly stringent arts funding climate at the time, imaginative ideas, such as the Poetry Society scheme to offer a poet in school via the Internet (Harries, 1983: 7), and the evolution of unforeseen funding partnerships, continued to open up new possibilities for exploration and debate.

The Education Officer/Department

Parallel to the development of the residency concept an increasing number of art galleries, orchestras, theatres and museums began appointing education officers who had the skills to liaise between the arts establishment and schools, initiate new patterns of collaboration and partnership and provide a range of stimulating contexts in which children, teachers and artists could interact. Once again the Gulbenkian Foundation played a significant role through, for example, funding an Education and Community Officer at London's Whitechapel Gallery in 1977.

The Drumcroon Education Art Centre in Wigan opened in 1980 and pioneered an approach which sought to place artists in every school in the LEA. The Centre and the Artist in Wigan Schools Scheme was a collaboration between Drumcroon, Wigan Education Authority, the Art Adviser, local artists, schools and children, with the Gulbenkian Foundation again playing a facilitating role. Through the Schools Loan Service (Taylor, 1991: 7) all schools could also have access to original works of art and through the involvement of the Turnpike Gallery there were two centres for visits, exhibitions and workshops. The scheme was based on partnership and it is worth quoting the policy statement at some length:

'To give all Wigan's young people - irrespective of age -their teachers and the local community access to the range, breadth and variety of the visual arts through the main focus of contemporary makers, taking into account such issues as race, gender and special needs. To give further insight and understanding , the Centre provides its visitors with opportunity to engage in practical activities and it attempts to place each exhibition in a contextual framework by demonstrating process through resident artists and craftspeople and through the use of secondary source material which has the potential to range across time, place and cultures' (Taylor, 1991: 9).

In its integration of education at the heart of gallery programme planning, Drumcroon created a model of practice that was way ahead of its time and has been a source of ongoing inspiration to many artists and teachers.

Developments

Involvement of many larger arts companies with schools was, no doubt, originally conceived as a marketing device to encourage 'bums on seats' or equivalent. Nevertheless, many arts organisations were genuinely keen to access a wider constituency to the world of the arts and explore ways of achieving the intention in practice. For example, orchestras such as Northern Sinfonia noted that they contained smaller ensembles within themselves that could function autonomously in an educational context. In Leicestershire musicians were commissioned to work alongside young people in youth and school orchestras.

Richard McNichol, with the Apollo Trust, pioneered a particular style of children's concert (McDonald, 1980: 11). This consisted of a developmental series of concerts, complete with follow-up material for the classroom, which actively involved children in composing, playing instruments and conducting.

In dance, companies such as the London Contemporary Dance Theatre evolved teaching programmes which frequently had a direct relationship to a given performance. This involved classes of children, teachers and adults in a wider community setting and could be spread over several developmental stages. Tensions developed with funding bodies such as the Arts Council which traditionally saw the resourcing of school-based work as the obligation of the education authority, not the arts funder. Some teachers also expressed concern that what was being taught could be done more effectively by themselves rather than the dancer as artist/teacher. However, when the package was a comprehensive mixture of residency, performance, workshops and classes, the resulting experience could be a profound one for pupil and teacher alike.

Mainstream arts companies related to schools in a variety of ways. Workshops, theatre days, follow-up notes and resources were created, focusing on current presentations or performances. Actors, directors, musicians, painters have held audience discussions; backstage and gallery visits have been organised. Some theatres mounted shows specifically aimed at school audiences. The larger national companies such as the RSC and the Royal Opera evolved sophisticated Education Departments with impressive programmes of workshops, presentations and performances specially aimed at schools, tours, visits and work pack materials.

Some forward-looking theatres went as far as to set up companies of actors specifically committed to work in local schools.

The Arts in Schools, the Gulbenkian report of 1982, commenting on the activities of theatre-in-education companies, observed:

> 'Their work represents the most sustained and perhaps the most far-seeing attempts so far to harness the capabilities and resources of professional artists to the purposes of education' (Robinson, 1982: 114).

The growth of theatre in education

TIE, as it has become known, emerged as a definable movement during the sixties (Jackson, 1993). Its unique nature lay in the sophisticated relationships it evolved with its audiences, subject material, teachers and theatre form which frequently involved structured, active participation. The Belgrade Theatre in Coventry pioneered the movement from 1965 in a bid to redefine the Theatre's roots in the community and to provide access for people of all ages to appropriate and good arts practice and experience. The emphasis was on the power of drama/theatre as an educational medium and a force for change. The concept of the TIE 'programme' was established, which in principle included a preliminary teachers' workshop, support materials, the company visit and a follow-up process. Some of the better-resourced companies had their own education officers who liaised between company and schools.

Art or education?

Although there was a rapid growth of activity in the seventies there was a tension between arts funders, education authorities and the nature of the work. Theatre-in-education programmes usually focused on issues considered to be of contemporary significance to the audience. The depth of research, debate and devising involved in the process placed a strong emphasis on the content of a programme. Funding bodies such as the Arts Council, with their stated intention to 'develop and improve knowledge, understanding and practice of the arts' (McDonald, 1980: 25), felt that such companies were more concerned with education than with art. Situations occurred in which the Arts Council or Regional Board argued that the TIE company should be funded by the LEA because their work was primarily 'education', and the LEA argued that the work was primarily 'art' and should be supported by the Arts funders.

Originally, TIE companies were set up from within mainstream theatres such as in Leeds, Bolton and Lancaster. Variations on this theme arose as independent companies grew up with their own company and charitable status. Attachment to a theatre company can bring huge benefits in terms of access to back-up facilities and resources. However, the attachment can be a mixed blessing when the theatre company itself is under pressure. As the experience of recent years has shown, the TIE company then becomes vulnerable and exposed to cuts.

Professional organisation

The TIE movement also produced a professional organisation, the Standing Conference of Young People's Theatre (SCYPT), established in 1975, which provided a challenging and sometimes turbulent forum for the discussion and development of the theory and practice of Young People's Theatre. SCYPT publishes a regular journal and promotes an annual conference. The actors' union, Equity, also recognised TIE as a unique branch of the arts 'industry' and helped to formalise contractual guidelines.

Other developments

Some dance companies have operated in the same way as TIE companies. Ludus Dance Company was set up to help young people become more aware, through dance, of important contemporary issues. As in TIE each performance is ideally backed up with previews for teachers, workshops and follow-up materials.

The Cockpit Arts Workshop in London was established in 1970 by the Arts Inspectors within the Inner London Education Authority (I.L.E.A.). There were teams of professional workers in theatre, visual arts and music who were responsible to the relevant subject inspector. For example, the opera team employed young singers to create presentations based on specific operas which were then toured to schools (Tambling, 1997: 44).

A number of children's theatre companies emerged across the country specialising in touring schools with plays for young people. These ranged from highly professional groups committed to providing work of the highest quality, to companies who earned a reputation for exploiting children and young actors alike. There were also a growing number of puppet theatre companies who had to struggle hard to gain recognition within the wider theatre frame.

Community and cross-cultural arts

The growth of community arts was inspired by a wish to create bridges between people, the communities in which they lived and the arts. The movement was inspired by the belief that art belongs to all people without prejudice. The work of some community artists included work in schools and demonstrated the potential of the arts to draw school and community closer together. In *Artists and People* (1978) Sue Braden recognises the importance of training. Whilst acknowledging the shifts in perspective that were enabling more artists to work in a range of educational and community settings she noted:

> 'Relatively few of the artists whose practice is documented in this report had any sort of theoretical perspective which they could draw on when working in these new contexts. In most cases their academic training gave them little more than some basic technical know-how. We should not be surprised, therefore, that many of them found the experience of working outside the structures for which they had specifically trained has resulted in a great many difficulties and false starts' (Braden, 1978: 7).

The first training scheme aiming to give artists the specific skills needed to work in schools was at Leicester Polytechnic (now De Montfort University) in 1991. Since then a wide range of initiatives has been developed (see Chapter 3, A Survey of the Current Situation).

The animateur

In the early eighties some regional arts boards and local authorities employed 'animateurs' who would be resident in a specific area or community. Their task was to stimulate, encourage and involve people directly in arts practices. They were usually skilled in some specific art form and worked as practical, hands-on arts development officers. Their brief usually included involvement with schools, colleges and youth centres. For example, in 1982 an animateur was appointed by South West Arts to work in Restormel, Cornwall. The animateur was a writer and theatre director. He used these skills to initiate an ambitious community play. The performance, at a local secondary school, involved professional and amateur artists and became a focus for training and further arts educational developments.

Outside school

The activities of youth orchestras and youth theatres began increasingly to involve young people in arts activities outside of school hours. They provided creative channels for those with a passion for theatre and music, as well as those for whom the formal structures of school did not encourage confidence and expression. Such activities created unique opportunities for young people of different backgrounds and experience to share and work together. Organisations such as the National Youth Theatre were national manifestations of this development. At a local level youth theatres were very dependent on the energies of individuals and were not embedded in the ethos of wider youth provision. All too often when the key individual left the scene the activity ceased. In contrast, youth orchestras were originally established alongside instrumental tuition services to provide opportunities for performing and a progressive 'ladder' towards excellence.

In the early eighties the Arts Council set up Arts in Education for a Multicultural Society (AEMS), a curriculum project putting anti-racist/multicultural policies into practice through workshops and in-service training in schools and colleges, led by practising professional black artists. The growth of artist representative bodies like the International Association of Theatre for Children and Young People (ASSITEJ) was also part of a growing recognition that the arts not only provided a context for exploring specific issues and experiences, but also, by nature of the aesthetic language of the arts themselves, offered a vehicle for challenging prejudices and encouraging cross-cultural dialogue and understanding. Sita Brahmachari observes:

> 'As well as enormously extending the breadth of students' knowledge and understanding of their subject, a drama curriculum which explores the aesthetics of multiculturalism may bring us as teachers closer to our aim of countering racial myopia than the issue-based drama of the past. While the latter set out to challenge stereotypical attitudes about race, the former encourages students to explore and express distinct sensibilities, moving beyond the simple opposition of prejudice and oppression. An aesthetically grounded

multicultural curriculum offers students the conceptual and practical tools through which to explore and find their own creative space within a historical and cultural continuum (Brahmachari in Hornbrook, 1998: 33).

The changed landscape

Hey! You, what are you doing in here?
    Comment made by a teacher to an actor about to enter a classroom.

The above comment was addressed to an actor-in-residence in a school corridor. The scheme was part of a programme of diversification which Rent a Role at the Plymouth Barbican Theatre was undertaking and had been requested by a number of teachers in subjects ranging from science to history. One of the strengths of the project was the close working relationship and collaboration involving company, teachers and local authority advisory teachers. The latter, besides funding the operation, followed up individual sessions and helped to nurture an ongoing dialogue about the place of drama within the whole curriculum of the school. By the early nineties the funding and the advisory teachers' jobs had both been cut and systematic development of the partnership and skills involved had been curtailed.

The 1988 Education Reform Act

TIE – LMS – RIP (Atherton, 1991:17)

The work of arts-in-education companies has been severely affected by legislation introduced over the past two decades. Many of these companies received grant support from LEAs as part of the fabric of locally provided services. Local Management of Schools devolved resources to individual schools and many did not choose to spend money on the arts. Neither regional arts organisations nor the RABs were able or willing to make up the loss in grant, so many companies disappeared altogether (Jackson, 1993).

The devolution of budgets within Local Management of Schools made it difficult to continue LEA supported services such as artists in schools and music tuition programmes, youth orchestras and theatres, and arts education centres (Stephens in Lockwood (Ed), 1997:6). There is no doubt that this was a frustrating and difficult time for many artists involved in education. However, despite the overall gloomy picture there were examples of LEAs, for example, Leeds and Birmingham, holding on to and actually expanding their support services. In Leeds an impressive range of well-resourced and well-planned projects was made available to schools through the Leeds Artists in Schools Programme. A central intention of the programme was to enable 'schools make the running in identifying the purposes for which they wish to develop a relationship with an artist' (Downing, 1996: 22).

In drama, music and dance, pressure on core funding led to a shift away from participatory projects and an increase in the number of 'performance only pieces' for larger audiences

(Jackson, 1993:26). This was seen by many artists as a triumph of quantity over quality. Participatory programmes continued to be developed by the more secure companies or those that managed to negotiate new, more diverse funding bases.

The National Curriculum

The demands of the National Curriculum, the pressures and priorities it created, influenced how teachers judged the relevance and appropriateness of using an artist or artists. In 1973 the Gulbenkian Foundation suggested that teachers use artists to step out of the formal, examination-based curriculum to take a wider 'humanistic' view of education. In a more prescriptive teaching environment this detachment is not so easy to facilitate. Hence many artists have sought to understand more about how their own work can relate directly to the demands of the curriculum and the immediate concerns of teachers.

The Education Reform Act of 1988 outlined the need for a broad curriculum. Section 2 requires that the promotion of pupils' 'spiritual, moral, cultural, mental and physical development' has a central place. The curriculum must also 'prepare pupils for the opportunities, responsibilities and experiences of adult life'.

Exposure to the arts is obviously linked to the status of specific art forms within the National Curriculum. Art and music are foundation subjects from Key Stage 1 to 3, with drama, literature and media education being a requirement within the standing orders for English. Dance, within physical education, is a requirement up to Key Stage 2.

Although the National Curriculum is set out in terms of specific subjects there is scope, under the Education Act (No2) 1986 and the Education Reform Act of 1988, for the headteacher and governing body to choose how to organise the curriculum in order to meet the basic aims. This includes choices as to how much time should be allocated for each subject, how much money spent and what teaching methods to use.

The school context

From Key Stage 4 the arts are an optional, rather than compulsory part of the National Curriculum. This position highlights their vulnerability. It is possible for student teachers to begin their professional training having had little contact with the arts since they themselves were at Key Stage 3. The contribution of the artist from outside the school builds on and enhances the arts work within a school. At the Opera and Music Theatre Forum in November 1994 Jo Shapcott commented:

> 'We are on the boundary between professional arts and arts education in schools. Our work has to operate with the framework of full educational provision – enhancing it rather than filling gaps in basic provision' (Rogers, 1995: 18).

Artists in schools projects are most effective when there is a good arts teaching foundation within the school. The training of specialist teachers of the arts in Britain has a deservedly high reputation, though the position of the arts in the National Curriculum has created considerable anxiety. For instance, the suggestion by the Teacher Training Agency (1998), that trainee teachers undertaking PGCE courses in drama should follow the Initial Teacher Training National Curriculum for English, could lead to a fall in the standards of specialist drama teaching.

Concern has been expressed by many involved in promoting and delivering the work of artists in schools that a growing number of teachers have had limited training in the arts (Rogers, 95:18, RSA, 1997: 125, Trowsdale, 1997: 3-4). The Royal Society for the Arts has recently commissioned a review of the current state of the arts in teacher training and development, particularly for primary school teachers.

Responding to the changed landscape

Arts Education Agencies

The idea of the Arts Education agency is relatively new. It has been developed to provide information, networking and advice to schools interested in working with artists. The loss of central advisory services and the devolution of budgets created a need for such intermediary support. Some agencies have arisen from within an LEA context whilst others operate independently in collaboration with one or more RABs.

The Paul Hamlyn Foundation initiated a research programme to look at the development of agencies in 1991 (Harries and Shaw, 1991). Four years later a report commissioned by the Arts Council observed that their development was 'erratic', though a small number of agencies had become well established and effective local and regional resources (Harries and Shaw, 1995). Despite this uneven start, agencies continued to emerge across the country in a range of forms and partnerships with LEAs, RABs, national and local foundations and schools. In 1995 the Arts Council set up the Arts Education Agencies Development Initiative which provided one-year funding to encourage the development of good models of agency practice. The Initiative described agencies as:

> 'A range of organisations whose principal remit is to act as brokers between professional artists and the education sector. Their aim is to promote a higher standard and a more equitable spread of arts education for all, in partnership with schools and the professional arts community. Their function may include: administering an artist's residency, advice, information and training, but will not include direct work with participants' (ACE, 1995).

Cumbria Arts in Education is an example of an agency set up in 1992. It is an independent agency although it was set up by a partnership of county council, district councils and Northern Arts to take a major responsibility for arts education in Cumbria. The agency's education brief includes taking a strategic overview of work in the county, identifying gaps in provision, and seeing where the curriculum offers opportunities for creative and innovative exploration. Most projects are initiated by schools although some 'strategic projects' are also promoted, resourced and co-ordinated. An example of the latter is a musician in residence project that made a percussionist and composer available to a large number of schools.

Warwickshire LEA and County Council have, for almost a decade, directed funds to an artists team: one and a half full-time staff dedicated to liaison between artists and schools. This includes the running of INSET programmes and the promotion of work in a range of art forms in nursery, primary, secondary and special schools. Other outstanding examples of productive partnership will be outlined in more detail in Chapter Three.`

A major challenge facing those agencies that do not have roots in an LEA is the development of planning, monitoring and evaluation programmes that enhance quality of provision as well as providing an information and networking service. In the past, well-informed advisory teachers played an invaluable role in this and it is important that such expertise is not replaced with less rigorous and critical support.

The Lottery

Initially the Lottery only supported capital projects but more recently, through its Arts for Everyone scheme, it has widened the scope of giving to include revenue support and other categories. The Arts for Everyone scheme included an 'Express' component in which smaller community and educational organisations could apply for resources to carry out a specific project. In many instances this involved schools working directly with artists. The tension between quality of provision and entitlement for the many emerges repeatedly throughout this review. Arts for Everyone may indeed provide a valuable taster experience for many groups and individuals, but there is a danger of promoting expectations which cannot be met. Unless the initial experience can be evaluated, built upon and developed there is a real possibility that the end result will be frustration for the many with little longer-term benefit for anyone.

As yet, the Lottery has not systematically been used to address the single most pressing issue facing many arts organisations: the problem of basic core funding. However, it has become an increasingly prominent feature of the arts funding landscape. A senior officer from South West Arts explained that his RAB spends over 60% of staff time on Lottery related issues. There is growing concern that it is being seen as a sort of financial *deus ex machina* that can descend from above and resolve the difficulties and complexities of the arts world.

On a more positive note, the role of the Regional Arts Boards as key gatekeepers to the Lottery has helped to raise their profile and accessibility, even though the process has stretched their resources to the limits.

Dancing with the agencies

The recognition by agencies such as Health and Police that the arts are a powerful vehicle for learning has led, over recent years, to a growth in arts work on such issues as HIV/AIDS, drugs and bullying. Some companies call themselves Arts in Health Education companies and, in the area of drama, the Theatre in Health Education Trust has been set up to promote such work.

The backing for this type of activity arose out of a sense of urgency surrounding HIV/AIDS related issues and the demand for imaginative ways of communicating the seriousness of the problem. Health authorities were looking for ways of making meaningful contact with young people and the arts seemed to provide a ready-made vehicle. There is some evidence, reported in discussion with health officers who have funded arts in health programmes over the past ten years, that the level of funding for this type of work has levelled off but many authorities are still actively supporting projects on issues such as drug abuse, child protection, autocrime and bullying (Cook, 1996).

The Whitechapel Gallery is 'the gallery with the longest history of working with professional visual artists in education' (Burgess in Prentice (ed.), 1995: 121). Having lost a core LEA grant the Gallery had to develop a more diverse funding base. The Gallery is situated on the edge of the City of London and this made it possible to tap into development funds such as Docklands Development and City Challenge. This has extended the range of the Gallery's community involvement in environmental and public art programmes. It has also introduced the interest of the sponsor as a key factor in planning.

Sponsorship

Commercial sponsorship and support of the arts has grown hugely. The value of business sponsorship grew from £600,000 in 1976 to nearly £83 million in 1994-5 (Department of National Heritage (DNH), 1997). Companies such as Marks and Spencer, Sainsbury's and W.H.Smith have been very involved in promoting arts education programmes for many years.

Businesses have supported arts in education programmes in a number of ways, from straight 'giving', commercial sponsorship – which is seen as a two-way exchange of benefit – and help in kind, which may include, for example, assistance in printing programmes.

The intention initially was that such support would be an 'extra'. During the eighties and early nineties, for example, Rent a Role at the Plymouth Barbican Theatre received generous, ongoing support from Marks and Spencer. However, as the years went on the theatre company was faced with continuing standstill grants from the arts funding bodies and the sponsorship support became essential to cover basic running costs.

The Association for Business Sponsorship of the Arts (ABSA)

The Association for Business Sponsorship of the Arts (ABSA) is an agency that seeks to promote partnerships between the private sector and the arts. It was set up in 1976 and by 1996 it had over 300 member companies. The Association runs a pairing scheme which matches a percentage of a sponsor's investment in a particular project. *Setting the Scene* includes the following observation:

'There are no detailed figures for the level of sponsorship that goes on arts education. However it is clear that sponsorship plays a substantial role in funding educational projects in both arts organisations and schools. For example, many arts organisations can only fund their own educational projects with some element of sponsorship: and one national survey suggests that up to a third of schools rely on business sponsorship for extra-curricular activities' (DNH, 1997: 44).

The growing demand for evaluation

In the sixties and seventies the work of artists in schools was predominantly supported through partnerships involving local education authorities and the regional arts boards. Arts officers and advisers played an important role in facilitating this process. The artist or company would have to justify their activities to these key personnel who already had a professional understanding of what the work was about. In the eighties this picture changed dramatically. The more stringent financial climate meant that RABs were operating standstill budgets at best. Coupled with inflation this inevitably led to an increase in costs for artists and, consequently, cutbacks in provision.

However, also during the eighties, other players entered the scene such as health authorities and the 'heritage industry'. Several health officers recognised that the arts were a valuable resource for promoting health and well-being. They were increasingly willing to develop the idea but had to justify their intentions to hard-headed financial controllers who wanted identifiable outcomes for the investment. Tony Jackson of Manchester University, in his paper 'Anecdotes are no longer enough' (Jackson, 1995) called for greater rigour from artists and companies in the evaluation of their work as a matter of urgency. The difficulty would be finding ways of evaluating arts processes that did justice to their intentions and did not distort the integrity of the activities for the sake of locating readily identifiable outcomes. In this, as Tony Jackson observed, 'academic research has a vital role to play in identifying, testing and (where appropriate) helping to implement models of evaluative methodology that will be of benefit to companies, funders and, most of all, to potential audiences of the work' (Jackson, 1995: 1).

Summary of chapter

Over many years artists have brought a diverse range of creative activity into schools. In the sixties and seventies this activity became focused in such developments as residencies, the establishment of education officers and departments in orchestras, galleries, theatres and museums, the emergence of arts companies dedicated to education and the work of community artists.

Funding patterns were established which usually involved LEAs and the RABs and significant charitable foundations such as Calouste Gulbenkian. Events during the eighties and nineties had a major impact on these developments. In particular the Education Reform Act, with the introduction of the National Curriculum, led to some schools placing a reduced emphasis on the development of the arts within their planning and budgeting. Local Management of Schools profoundly affected the position of the LEA as funder and adviser. This led to major cutbacks to services such as theatre in education and instrumental music tuition.

As a result various initiatives evolved to replace the previous support structures and create new mechanisms of support. Artists began working with a range of agencies, the Lottery allowed funding of education projects and arts organisations were encouraged to seek commercial sponsorship. Education agencies began to appear as brokers between artists and schools.

In an increasingly stringent and competitive funding climate there developed an urgent need to establish more rigorous evaluation procedures to justify funding.

2 A Survey of the current situation

Leading through Learning

'There has been a huge growth in educational activity by artists and arts organisations – not only those specifically set up to carry out education work but also those, such as galleries and performing companies, where education is part of a wider remit.' (ACE, 1997: 8).

'Arts Education in schools has suffered from the decline in central services provided by local authorities and the fact that the arts are an optional part of the curriculum above age 14' (ACE, 1997: 3).

The above quotes are from *Leading through Learning*, the Arts Council's 1997 policy document for Education and Training. They reveal two contradictory trends and developments which artists who work in education have experienced over recent years:

- a significant increase in the educational activities of arts organisations funded through the Arts Council of England (ACE) and Regional Arts Boards (RABs)

- the virtual disappearance of committed educational art forms such as theatre in education.

The last few years have seen significant statements of intention from the Department of National Heritage (DNH, now re-named The Department for Culture, Media and Sport, DCMS) and ACE regarding education and wider youth arts provision. In 1996 the DNH published *Setting the Scene* in which we find that: 'All children and young people should have wide-ranging opportunities, within school and outside, to enjoy the arts as a spectator and as a performer, creator or maker' (DNH, 1996: 8). The document 'starts from the fundamental principle that good-quality arts should be open to all, and that everyone should have the chance to take part in them' (DNH, 1997: 5).

The Arts Council's *Leading through Learning* states that 'enabling everyone to enjoy, derive inspiration from, and participate in the arts is the core mission of the integrated Arts Council/RAB arts funding system in all regions and all art forms' (ACE, 1997: 3).

The same document also claims: 'There has been a huge growth in educational activity by artists and arts organisations – not only those specifically set up to carry out education work but also those, such as galleries and performing companies, where education is part of a wider remit' (ACE,1997: 3). The document does not actually provide evidence for this conclusion and some artists and arts officers dispute the claim. The contradictions in themselves show that fragmentation is one of the key features of the current artists-in-schools landscape. In some areas the work is thriving, in others, for a variety of social, political and educational reasons, there is little going on.

We can look at the current situation in more detail under the following headings:

- The educational activities of ACE- and RAB-funded organisations.

- Specialist arts in education companies/groups.

- Freelance artists/groups with an interest in education.

- Working in partnership.

The Educational activities of ACE and RAB funded organisations

In 1997 the Arts Council published a report, *Arts Organisations and their Educational Programmes*, which surveyed the educational work of organisations funded by ACE and the RABs. The report covered such areas as funding, types of activity, staffing and evaluation. The report revealed that 78% of these organisations had educational programmes, 63% with dedicated officers running them. The aims of the report were to 'build up an understanding of the range and types of educational programmes, to provide firm data for the purposes of policy development and advocacy and to establish the first national database of arts organisations and their educational programmes' (Hogarth, Kinder and Harland, 1997: 6).

The Arts Council report outlines the number of companies with education policies. It provides a wealth of information and useful statistics regarding the wide range of educational activities carried out by theatres, orchestras, galleries, museums and art centres.

The reasons for this 'growth' in education activity may be linked to the increased expectations from arts funding bodies that clients receiving public funds should develop educational policies and activities, demands in the National Curriculum for cultural provision in schools, and, working in tandem with both the above, the rather mercurial impact of the Lottery.

Headteachers have been keen to satisfy governors that their schools are catering for the 'cultural development' of their pupils. Visits from artists and visits to theatres, museums and galleries seem an obvious way of meeting this requirement. Many schools take full advantage of such opportunities. However, evidence from inspectors, advisers and arts officers, as well as artists, shows that some schools have sought to satisfy the demands for 'cultural development' without feeling the need to explore the experience in any greater depth or integrate it into the wider curriculum. A draft QCA guidance paper comments:

> 'Providing cultural events and experiences may not in itself enable cultural development. It is in the critical analysis, evaluation and reflection which follow the experiences where cultural development occurs. It is also in the recognition of how the pupil can contribute to, and engage with, the various cultures within which they live' (QCA, 1997).

Saville Kushner has researched how the work of artists in schools is perceived by children (Kushner, 1991). His research illustrates the potentially contrasting perceptions of an arts experience by children, teachers and artists. Its implications are important in helping teachers identify appropriate artists and projects that meet the needs of specific groups of children.

Another recent Arts Council document, *The Heart of the Matter* (Rogers, 1997), moves the debate forward and acknowledges that, whilst a growing number of arts organisations are genuinely keen to increase the level of their educational activity, fewer are actually beginning to build education into the core of their policies and activities. Subtitled 'The Education Research and Development Initiative (ERDI): its impact and implications for the future', the report reflects the Arts Council's intention to 'promote the value of an integrated education programme, the positive effects it can have on the whole culture of an organisation, and the benefits it offers potential audiences' (Rogers, 1997: 2).

In its first year 23 arts organisations were awarded grants. The organisations ranged from the Arnolfini Gallery in Bristol to the London based Poetry Society. One of the basic approaches used, for example, by the Cheltenham International Festival of Music, was to research specific existing education work and explore the potential to link it with the wider programme. Another approach, for example, by the London International Festival of Theatre (LIFT), was to look at the organisation itself and its staff to identify and encourage opportunities for development, involvement and training. *The Heart of the Matter* offers

> 'the opportunity to carry out a one-year research and development initiative to review the place of education within the organisation; devise strategies which link education more effectively with other aspects of their work; explore the impact of education work on the development of the artform and the individual artist; and stimulate debate on the key role that education plays in ensuring that arts organisations are accessible' (Rogers, 1997: 2).

The ERDI initiative does seem to have had some success in bringing education into a more central position within the organisations involved. Literature organisations seem to have especially benefited. For example, the Arvon Foundation is now planning to put courses for teachers and trainee teachers at the centre of its work. As Brian Cox, Chair of the Arvon Foundation, commented: 'My dream is that it will soon be possible for all teacher-trainees to attend Arvon-style courses in writing, and that this will release a great surge of creative energy in our schools' (Rogers, 1997: 39).

In Chapter two it was acknowledged that some arts organisations saw education as primarily a marketing device to attract new audiences. The ERDI report comments:

> 'The South Bank Centre's Head of Education, Gillian Moore, talks of the need to become 'creatively honest'. This process was played out at the start of the collaboration between education and marketing at Warwick where education at first queried marketing's use of superlatives and lack of questioning while marketing bridled at education's idiosyncrasies and lack of clarity. Now they understand each other's objectives very well and share the language' (Rogers, 1997: 27).

Diversification and expansion

'I view the orchestra as an ensemble of possibilities that does not exclude anything.'
Pierre Boulez (Renshaw, 1995: 254).

The Arts Council's chartered objectives are to 'develop and improve the knowledge, understanding and practice of the arts' and to 'increase the accessibility of the arts to the public' (Macdonald, 1980: foreword). It is in pursuit of these objectives that the Council's Education and Training Department has been encouraging arts organisations to widen the frame of reference within which they operate. A recent research project, carried out by the National Foundation for Educational Research for the Arts Council, explores the aims and rationales of education programmes currently being developed by orchestras. An introductory leaflet by the NFER comments:

> 'This recent proliferation of orchestral educational programmes has been underpinned by a belief that the survival of the orchestra is dependent on a shift in its professional culture and a diversification of its role. Without negating its traditional roles, it was widely felt that the orchestra should expand its existing sphere of work and become a creative, flexible ensemble with a range of activity that is not only more relevant to the cultural needs of the wider community but also central to its own artistic development' (NFER, 1997: 1).

Ernest Fleischman, Managing Director of the Los Angeles Philharmonic Orchestra, observes:

> 'An orchestra is a 'community of musicians' who can provide a jazz band, an early music ensemble or a contemporary music group, as well as acting as a single symphony orchestra' (Renshaw, 1995: 254).

This thinking is reflected, for example, in the educational approach of the London Symphony Orchestra. The orchestra has a staff of seven in its education department and educational work represents a significant part of the contractual obligations of musicians. The London Sinfonietta focuses on contemporary music and also employs musicians and composers who have the flexible skills to move between concert hall and school.

Developments in GCSE, the impact of Local Management of Schools, the National Curriculum and the shortage of music teachers have also led to an increased demand and pressure for orchestras to become more directly involved in education. This has been observed especially in relation to composition. 'Performing and Composing' is included in the National Curriculum music requirements. According to *Musicians Go To School* many primary school teachers are likely to seek general support, whereas secondary school music specialists are more likely to seek help in meeting specific deficiencies:

> 'Their requirements are likely to focus upon developing pupils' skills in composition and in broadening the range of pupils' musical experience to embrace other musical traditions, including non-European music' (Prattley, Rhydderch and Stephens, 1993: 7).

The shrinking of the music advisory service has reinforced this trend. The Teacher Training Agency includes music as a 'shortage subject' from September 1998.

The Royal Shakespeare Company has been running a KS3 project with workshops and courses across the country. The project seeks to develop techniques and approaches that will help to make Shakespeare's plays accessible to children of all abilities. A week-long summer school for teachers is a central part of the wider project. This is a good example of how a large arts organisation can respond directly to the needs of the curriculum. The National

Theatre's primary school Shakespeare project, focusing on literacy development, is another.

Southern Arts and Eastern Arts have produced a valuable set of guidelines to help arts organisations write an education policy and strategy but, as the authors of the document observe, arts organisations must be ready and willing to take the idea on board. They comment:

> 'Before you begin, ask yourself, your senior manager(s) and your Board whether your organisation is ready to write an education policy. You will need to establish the needs and interests of the local community and to try out a range of approaches before you can formulate a policy' (Bryant and Dust, 1997: 1).

Specialist arts in education companies/groups

Drama, through theatre in education, has been the most extensively represented art form in the world of small-scale, dedicated arts companies. During the sixties and seventies TIE emerged as a discernible 'movement' and a forceful focus for debate. However, there are also companies in other art forms that work extensively in education. For example, companies such as Folkworks in the North and The Wren Trust in the South West, have taken up references to folk music in the National Curriculum and used this to develop a portfolio of work with schools (Department of Education, (Music) 1995: 6).

There is also some evidence from arts education agencies that groups of visual artists are collaborating to share studio space and offering schools group projects. This development has been influenced by the pioneering work of centres such as Drumcroon and innovative approaches to teacher training in the area of art and design at, for example, the University of Central England, Manchester Metropolitan University and University College, Chester.

The outlook for some of the older, specialist arts in education companies, whose funding patterns developed in a different political climate, is less encouraging. In the world of TIE, for example, well-established companies serving school communities in Manchester, Leeds, Lancaster, Coventry, London, Harlow and elsewhere have all but disappeared. In some key instances, where a TIE company has been a part of a regional theatre such as in Leeds and Coventry, the service it provided has been absorbed into an expanded education department.

Theatre companies experience particular problems in representing themselves to schools, which arise from the nature of the art form itself. Running a theatre company is expensive and it is not practical to create a completely different production for each school - despite the impressive range of flexible techniques evolved over the past thirty years. This means that schools are less proactive in determining the content than if they themselves commissioned, for example, a single visual artist. Theatre programmes for schools are frequently agenda led and, usually after extensive research, the product is then promoted to schools. The clearly identifiable agenda may not match an individual school's arts development plans. On the other hand the more abstract nature of dance and music allow for greater flexibility.

Redefining roles

The pressure to find resources from a range of sources has led to some companies diversifying their activities, redefining their role and integrating their work into a wider community framework. This may, for example, mean working in partnership with a local health authority to deliver an arts-based drugs project or working with police and probation authorities to devise a programme on autocrime issues. The Theatre in Health Education Trust has developed to support such theatre-based projects through fund raising, advocacy and training. There are also examples of new partnerships arising with groupings of schools and colleges of further and higher education.

Cross-arts developments

In recent years innovative arts companies such as DV8, the Kosh and The Right Size have explored the interconnections, shared vocabularies and dynamics of word, sound, rhythm, colour and shape. Musicians, actors, dancers, writers and visual artists have worked together in integrated creative processes in which art form boundaries have been extended and crossed. Many teachers of the arts have been inspired by such developments, which have enabled them to initiate debate in their schools about the relationship of the expressive arts to each other and their contribution to the academic and cultural life of the school.

Advantages and disadvantages

Working in partnership with a range of agencies has enabled some companies to survive and, in some cases, to continue using participatory methods of work with relatively small audience groups. Working in the maelstrom of multi-agency funding is also helping to give some companies greater status and access to the corridors of power in the city or town hall.

However, artists and arts administrators report problems facing arts companies in the changed landscape. These problems include concern over the loss of participatory arts skills, the fear that arts projects will become finance led with their content dictated by the needs of whichever agencies hold the purse strings, and the sheer amount of administrative time involved in negotiating with complex bureaucratic entities. Artists are concerned that their artistic integrity may be put at risk unless there is a genuine overlap of interest between themselves, schools and funding agencies.

Arts companies are currently seeking funds from a wide range of sources including foundations and trusts, such as Gulbenkian and Paul Hamlyn, businesses such as Marks and Spencer and Sainsbury's, and, as we have seen, government funds, such as the Single Regeneration Budget and the Lottery. Again the overall picture of provision is very patchy with an increasing number of companies affected by cutbacks to central funding bidding for resources for which there is spiralling demand.

The general view amongst practitioners, and one shared by many officers in the arts and education, is that legislation introduced over the past fifteen years has had a detrimental impact on the work of artists in schools. But this view is not unanimous. Dr Steve Ball,

Director of Catalyst TIE company in Birmingham, was a presenter at the Plymouth seminar 'Dancing with the Agencies', which examined new funding patterns and partnerships. He described how the work of Catalyst Theatre and its sister companies demands close working links with teachers and health authorities. The company has partnerships with 60 schools in Birmingham. Having lost their core funding they find that a climate has been created in Birmingham, through the vision of the LEA, that is conducive to the development of a range of artist-in-education projects. Through the Birmingham Primary Guarantee every school is encouraged to provide a professional arts experience for all its children. In Catalyst's experience LMS has led to schools having more money, protected by the LEA's agreements, available for the work of artists in schools.

Freelance artists with an interest in education

In some parts of the country the networking of the broader artistic community with the educational community has produced a fascinating variety of work and creative collaboration. Many examples abound and the Department of National Heritage's *Setting the Scene* documents several imaginative projects from towns, cities and villages across the country.

It is difficult to gain an overview of the activities of freelance artists who work on an occasional basis in schools. Most do not receive core funding and may not be members of a professional association. Their work covers a wide array of activities from pottery to poetry, from singing to bell ringing. In some parts of the country artists with experience in education may be included on the database of an arts in education agency. This is an important basic service provided by such agencies which are emerging as significant channels for networking, advice, training and funding.

Initiatives such as the Leeds Artists in Schools Programme are encouraging schools themselves to be more proactive in defining their own curricular needs in relation to input from artists (Downing, 1996: 15). The more expensive projects involving organisations such as the Royal National Theatre or the South Bank have usually been initiated by the arts organisations themselves (Pratley, Rhydderch and Stephens, 1993: 32).

There is a strong demand for the activities of freelance artists who can work effectively and flexibly in schools. Though many schools and LEAs are still keen to work with artists, the resources to fund more expensive arts in education inputs involving, for example, theatre or dance in education companies are not easily available. Poets, sculptors and others who tend to work individually, are discovering increasing opportunities to work in schools.

Artists have expressed concern over the impact of heavily subsidised companies, under pressure from The Arts Council, moving at an unprecedented speed into education and able to charge far less than the unsubsidised artist for workshop and other activities. They also market their educational work in attractive, glossy packages and publicity materials beyond the means of most freelance artists. This illustrates the need for an outside adviser, officer or agent who can link schools with the most appropriate artists for their specific needs.

Many musicians, and other artists, have a portfolio of work which may include a variety of activities from performing in an ensemble to a range of teaching commitments. Negotiating residencies in a range of contexts fits well into this pattern of employment; a pattern that is becoming more prevalent across the wider economy.

Professional support for artists

Artists who work extensively in schools comment on their sense of isolation. Membership of the Standing Conference of Young People's Theatre (SCYPT) has declined in recent years. The Association of Professional Theatre for Children and Young People (APT) has replaced SCYPT as a more popular forum for professional theatre in education workers. Dance companies that work extensively in education, such as Ludus and Green Candle, are also members of APT. Equity, the actors' union, has also played an important role in the 'industrial' development of TIE and has been prominent in resisting and opposing the closure of several companies throughout the country. The Independent Theatre Council (ITC) represents the interests of small-scale touring companies and is an invaluable source of advice for companies working in schools.

Arts workers in other art forms have not had the benefits of this degree of representation. The National Association for Music Education (NAME) is a valuable and growing networking body for music educators, but does not specifically represent the artistic and employment interests of professional musicians working in schools. The Incorporated Society of Musicians has been in existence since 1882 and has 47 centres across the country. The Society represents the interests of musicians in all areas of the profession. It provides a platform to express the views of the profession and plays an advocacy role in relation to, for example, current government legislation. The society also provides individual support in such matters as taxation and legal advice.

The National Society for Educators in Art and Design (NSEAD), is a 'learned society, subject association and trade union' (NSEAD,1997: 4). The society offers a general service to teachers of art, craft and design. Again it does not have a particular brief for the professional artist. For the last three years the Society, in partnership with the commercial company Berol (now Sanford UK), has been running a series of 'Artists Working With Teachers' workshops in centres across the country.

The National Association of Writers in Education (NAWE), incorporating the Verbal Arts Association, aims to represent and support writers, teachers and all those involved in the development of creative writing in education (NAWE, 1998). The NAWE Directory of Writers provides a detailed listing of member writers who are available for readings, workshops and placements.

Working in Partnership

Working in partnership has become the predominant way in which artist-in-school projects are funded. The impact of the Education Reform Act and cutbacks to the Arts Council, for example, made it unlikely that a local authority department could single-handedly fund an extensive artists-in-school programme. Lottery funding itself is based on the idea of partnership. New partnerships have arisen with LEAs, RABs and others to provide funding, information, training and evaluation.

Partnership is itself a complex issue. At the British Council Conference, 'Creative and Cultural Development', held during May 1998 in London, Dick Downing suggested four types of partnership involving artists and education:

- Supply-led, in which the arts organisation offers a 'product' or service to schools
- Demand-led, in which the school, with its own devolved budget, asks for a specific 'product' or service
- Overlapping agendas of interest, in which arts organisation and school negotiate from their respective standpoints
- Dynamic dialogue, in which the relationship is open-ended and involves a process of discovery and risk.

The majority of artist-in-schools projects have worked with the first, supply-led, model. When budgets were devolved to schools this created an opportunity for teachers to have a greater say in what projects they would like to have in school. However, unless schools are well informed about the availability and quality of provision the opportunity will not be fully exploited.

LEAs and artists in schools

In many parts of the country local education authorities no longer see themselves as front line providers for artists in schools. However, partnership between LEA, RAB and schools, or groups of schools, is a central feature of many current projects. The need for long-term planning, quality control and fund-raising makes partnership a basic necessity. For example, Dudley LEA has a scheme with West Midlands Arts Board that involves a three-way split of the cost of a project between LEA, RAB and school. If schools cannot raise their contribution, then there is a further fund to which they can apply for help.

Schools themselves are increasingly forming partnerships with other schools to help 'buy in' artists. In urban areas LEAs are increasingly looking to form partnerships with other LEAs. Advisers have commented that in order to move forward they, the LEAs, would have to think regionally. For example, the West Midlands Regional Arts Education Partnership involves twelve LEAs in an ambitious A4E Lottery bid for artists to work in schools.

Since greater budgetary responsibility now rests with individual schools many LEAs themselves do not have a clear overview of the degree of artist-in-schools activity within their own authorities. One LEA adviser commenting on his county's lack of an arts education policy observed: 'As a consequence the projects that have taken place over the years have tended to be beacons of excellence without an over-arching strategy'.

Artists and INSET

Artists in schools provide a range of specialist experiences for pupils that enhance the work of the classroom teacher. However, in order to maximise the use of limited resources, LEAs are increasingly focusing and prioritising their investments in artists on teachers themselves rather than emphasising the provision of an artistic experience for pupils. Several LEAs, for example, see the residency as a key strategy for teacher development. Others observe that they would be unlikely to fund a project unless there was a significant in-service component.

A number of LEAs have been involved in the setting up of education agencies to build up sources of information, networking and training. Some arts agencies have been initiated by a partnership of LEAs. For example, the Bolton, Bury and Rochdale Artists in School Agency arose from a pilot scheme in Bolton and has now attracted a major A4E Lottery award to carry out a programme over three years. The partners, which include private sponsors, the LEAs, ERDF funding, Bolton and Bury and Rochdale TECs and the Arts Council (through the Lottery) have raised around £0.5m for artists to work in schools over three years.

Another successful bid for Lottery funding, DAISI (Devon Artists in Schools Initiative), was initiated by the Devon Association of Governors and built up into a wide partnership involving Devon Curriculum Advice, Devon County Council Education Committee and the County Arts Officer.

Such partnerships are built on a recognition that longitudinal funding, i.e. planned and committed over a long period of time, must replace dependence on short-term projects and thinking.

RABs and artists in schools

The changed education landscape has put pressure on the RABs to take an increasingly proactive role in education. As the RABs have an umbrella responsibility for the development of the arts within their regions there is a growing demand for and pressure on them to evolve a strategy for education at all levels and to help build support and advisory structures. A recent addition to the pressure has been provided by the proposal of the current government that schools should provide an annual arts statement which shows what extra-curricular creative opportunities (ECCO) they provide.

The RABs recognise the need to develop a long-term, strategic view of the work of artists in education. For example, the London Arts Board (LAB), in responding to cutbacks to the extensive arts education services previously provided by the Inner London Education Authority, has supported, from its Arts Education Network funding programme, the establishment of arts education forums in 26 London Boroughs. More recently LAB extended this programme through the introduction of a three-year fund that a) targeted boroughs keen to evolve longer-term plans and b) encouraged closer partnerships between education and the business community. The scheme, London Arts Education Partnerships (LEAP), offers three years of funding to four London Boroughs per year on a rolling basis and creates an opportunity for longer-term planning and sustainability.

The development of LEAP was influenced by a project in Chicago called Creative Arts Partnership in Education (CAPE). CAPE has also been the inspiration for a major collaborative project in the north of England bringing together North West Arts Board, Yorkshire and Humberside Arts Board with Leeds and Manchester LEAs and schools.

CAPE was initially developed in Chicago in the early 1990s and has since spread across several states. The intention is to create partnerships between schools, artists and businesses which put creativity at the heart of their activity. The project is based on four principles:

- longevity; the programme is projected over seven years

- planning; allowing enough time for in-depth planning is essential

- evaluation; external evaluation is central from the beginning

- local control; emphasising local control at the point of delivery.

CAPE's programme in the north of England has already attracted large-scale resources from the Lottery and the Youthstart Programme of the European Social Fund.

RABs also have a crucial advocacy role and RAB education officers collaborate with colleagues to introduce education as a cross-curricular thread within all art form departments and encourage 'mainstream' RAB revenue-funded clients to develop education policies.

RABs and training

The RABs are aware that artists need training in order to work effectively in schools. Most of the RABs by themselves do not have sufficient resources to develop extensive training programmes. Eastern Arts set up a training course for artists and teachers with Anglia Polytechnic University. The course involved artists being paired with teachers and culminated in a residency at the teacher's school. Artists from a wide geographical area attended the course, which ran for over a year. Several working artists found a whole year's commitment financially difficult to sustain and there were also practical problems connected with transport.

Essex County Council, in collaboration with Eastern Arts Board, is developing the programme of study from the original Anglia Polytechnic University course. The course aims to train artists in the skills needed to set up projects and to give teachers the opportunity to work practically with artists on a residency project.

Over the past six years the London Arts Board has supported an 'Artists in Schools Training Course', which is an annual two-term accredited course in partnership with the London University Institute of Education. The course has evolved an accreditation process that is appropriate to the processes and skills involved and is not dependent solely on the written word. The course aims to provide artists with the information, understanding, confidence and skills that will help them to work successfully in a range of school contexts.

South West Arts has been involved with two initiatives seeking to encourage artists and teachers to collaborate together. One, at the University of the West of England, involves artists working on Initial Teacher Training programmes. Another, at The University College of St Mark and St John in Plymouth, centres on the development of a new artists-in-education programme on the College campus.

Evaluation

Evaluation is recognised as an essential part of a programme or project and most RABs have produced guidelines which are integrated into the process of grant application. These may involve artist, school and an outside perspective. The process is crucial for the ongoing development of good practice and should benefit artist, school, LEA and RAB.

There has been a great deal of uncertainty about the evaluation of artists in education projects. A joint initiative, involving the Arts Council and Regional Arts Boards, is currently being developed to address this issue. It is called the Evaluation Research and Development Initiative (Eastern Arts Board, 1998). The broad aim is to 'raise standards of practice in the evaluation of arts education projects across the arts, education and youth and community sectors by producing a practical evaluation resource containing accessible and easy-to-use materials' (Eastern Arts Board, 1998). The initiative aims to raise evaluation standards by:

- undertaking research to identify effective approaches to arts education evaluation
- producing an innovative, accessible and flexible evaluation resource for use by arts organisations, individual artists and the youth and community sectors
- running training sessions for target groups in how to use evaluation materials.

A handbook will be published later in 1998 after a lengthy and detailed research and development process.

The further growth of the arts education agency

The Arts Council's *Leading through Learning* identified the need to 'address gaps in the current provision of services by developing a network of arts education agencies across the country – and directly funding them where appropriate' (ACE,1997: 10). Rick Rogers, in *Developing Arts Education Agencies*, writes:

'Based on the work currently being carried out across the country, an arts education agency might be engaged in one or more of the following tasks:

- establishing, running and updating a database of artists to work in educational and community settings
- offering advice and expertise on arts education and related projects
- negotiating, setting up and/or running projects, such as artists' residencies or school/community events
- piloting innovative schemes and ideas to develop closer and more effective working relationships between artists and schools
- organising training courses for artists and teachers
- monitoring and evaluating the projects carried out
- administering grants for arts education projects

- identifying and negotiating new sources of income for such work

- providing a forum for discussion and exchange of information and practice

- carrying out lobbying and advocacy work for arts education.' (Rogers, 1998).

There are estimated to be over 60 agencies that fall within the definition of agency as perceived by ACE and the RABs. Such figures might imply a coherent network providing a high-quality service to schools and others. However, the Arts Council report *Developing Arts Education Agencies* shows that, whilst some areas benefit considerably from the existence of established agencies, coverage overall is patchy and the quality of provision variable (Rogers, 1998). Despite the uneven nature of provision the same report emphasises that enough has been learnt from a range of agency models over recent years to encourage and nurture the development of good practice more widely.

Maximising the impact: further observations on training

The relationship between artist and teacher is central to the development of good practice. That relationship can be enhanced with training on both sides and there are examples of practice around the country which provide useful models and ideas for debate and reference.

Students who take PGCE courses in art and design will have already undertaken an initial training in their subject. At the University of Central England the PGCE course is in the School of Art and Design Education, which is a part of the Faculty of Art and Design. This enables trainee teachers, who are artists in their own right, to maintain working links with practising artists who are not training to teach. The placement system for BA students means that a training artist's residency could coincide with a teacher training placement and that artist and teacher could collaborate. At University College, Chester, trainee teachers are introduced to their placement school as practising artists before they meet pupils in the role of teacher. The artist/teacher may, for example, have an exhibition of their own work at the school before beginning a teaching practice. Likewise at Manchester Metropolitan University students on the Art and Design PGCE work in groups in a school as artists in residence. Such schemes help students make 'the transition from the world of art and design to education – from professional artist to professional educator' (Burgess in Prentice (ed.), 1995: 113).

In a similar way student teachers at Warwick University, the University of Exeter, and the Central School of Speech and Drama will be directly involved in creating and presenting a theatre or music in education project in local schools as part of their course.

Bretton Hall College of the University of Leeds threads artists into several BA courses. For example, third year English specialists will work in collaboration with a practising writer. The College has also involved trainee teachers with the Royal Opera House's 'Write an Opera' course. This gives students contact with a range of artists and an opportunity to acquire skills that will be transferable and adaptable to their own school contexts.

Jo Trowsdale of Warwick University has examined 'the development of the artist as a pedagogic model' (Trowsdale, 1997: 34), a model which emphasises such qualities as individuality, communication, self-knowledge and the ability to think qualitatively (Parks, 1992: 54-6). Such thinking helps to break down barriers between artist and teacher and encourages teachers to respect and nurture their own creativity.

Training artists to work in schools

Different art forms demand a different balance of skills and temperament. At one end of the scale drama is a predominantly social activity whereas visual arts practice is more likely to be a private and solitary experience. In the world of music there is extensive debate about what skills a music graduate should have in order to meet the needs of the music profession – for example, the extent to which graduates should be skilled in composition, performance and leadership, have a wide understanding of repertoire and be skilled communicators. Peter Renshaw considers that:

> 'Although the climate is beginning to change, for many years music training has been bedevilled by a narrow view of technical excellence, which has resulted in artistic tunnel vision and a lack of concern for the creativity, flexibility and breadth of outlook that are necessary for music to be a living force in society' (Renshaw, 1995: 255).

The Guildhall School of Music and Drama in London runs a music in performance degree course to address this challenge. The directors of the course encourage artists to redefine their art in contemporary culture. The course involves developing the skills of composing and improvising, performances in schools and an extensive period of training in workshop skills. The course also encourages research and involvement in the field of instrumental learning and teaching.

In *Musicians Go To School* there is a recommendation for the training of musicians that raises key issues and is relevant for other art forms:

> 'In collaboration with the music and educational professions, a new programme of professional development should be initiated to provide professional performers with continuing opportunities to update knowledge and experience of developments in the education curriculum and classroom practice and to develop and refresh animation and teaching skills. The training programme should be open to all professional performers at any stage in their performance careers. It should combine formal teaching at a recognised centre for higher education and supervised projects in the classroom. It should be deliverable nationally and must therefore be of a modular construction. It should be validated and carry a recognised award. It should include a module on the use of new music technology' (Pratley, Rhydderch and Stephens, 1993: 40).

There are a number of courses and artist-in-education programmes across the country in such places as London, Cambridge, Bristol, Newcastle, Leeds, Lincoln, Warwick, Plymouth, Essex, Wakefield, Lancaster and elsewhere that could provide the first building blocks for such a vision.

Several of the larger-scale arts organisations themselves are increasingly running courses for their own staff in education though most are short-term based.

The overall current situation is fragmented and even displays contradictory developments. For example, an increase in education activity from mainstream arts organisations is counterbalanced by a decline in the activities of dedicated education companies such as in theatre in education.

Initiatives from the Arts Council such as ERDI (Rogers, 1997) have sought to encourage arts organisations to place education at the heart of their activities rather than on the periphery. This initiative has met with some success, especially with literary organisations. Some mainstream arts organisations are showing a willingness to diversify and work with greater flexibility. This would involve schools, as part of the wider community framework, more centrally in their activities. A number of initiatives have involved arts organisations directly in supporting delivery of aspects of the National Curriculum.

The work of dedicated arts education companies has been critically affected by legislation over the past two decades. Such companies have needed to diversify their activities in order to survive. This may mean working with a health or police authority, for example. There has also been a growth in cross-arts activities which cut across traditional art form boundaries. This has influenced the debate within schools regarding the place of the expressive arts within the wider curriculum.

It is not easy to gain a picture of the work of freelance artists who work in schools. Many are not core funded and, by definition, do not belong to an identifiable organisation. There would appear to be good opportunities for the individual artist who can negotiate a service and work flexibly with individual schools. Support for artists through professional associations is limited and many artists express a feeling of isolation.

Partnership is central to the development of good practice. LEAs are no longer front line providers for this work and see themselves working in partnership with the RABs and other partners to provide funding, information, evaluation and training. The RABs have an increasingly important role to play in education and have established some very constructive initiatives in areas such as regional development, evaluation and training. Arts education agencies have continued to develop and they are seen by the Arts Council as having considerable potential to broker relationships between education and the arts.

The relationship between artist and teacher is central to the development of good practice. That relationship can be enhanced with training on both sides and there are examples of practice around the country which provide useful models for debate and reference.

3 A Survey of Claims

'At the time you were there they were engaged.
They began to look, and to be interested.
They have grown.
Next time they have another experience they will be more aware.
They become obviously more alive' (Burroughs in Downing, 1996: 51).

As outlined in several publications over recent years (Sharpe and Dust, 1990: 140 – 143, Manser, 1995: 6) artists work practically with young people in schools in three essential ways:

- as maker – creating a piece of writing, sculpture or music

- as performer/presenter – presenting an exhibition, a performance of a play, piece of music or dance

- as teacher/facilitator – communicating skills, processes and generating interest and enthusiasm.

Artists also provide a stimulus for critical reflection – a professional performance or exhibition can encourage a critical response and deepen understanding of the processes involved.

A residency or other visit may work in a combination of the above. For example, TIE evolved participatory techniques for performance that sometimes involved all the above in one programme!

There are several ways in which an artist may interact with a school. The artist's visit may be for a single, one-off performance or presentation. At one extreme there is the 'bungee jump' encounter in which artist or company arrive at the school, present a play or recital and then depart leaving any follow-up work to be done solely by the teacher. At the other end of the spectrum a residency could involve teachers, artist and children working together over a whole school year.

The possibilities of different ways of working as maker, presenter or teacher, together with the range of alternative working models and structures within which children, artist and teacher meet, highlight the huge richness, diversity and potential of artists in schools as a resource for learning.

Over the years artists, teachers and other interested parties have had to persistently argue the case for the work in order to make it happen. Key foundations such as Gulbenkian have played a major role in the process; as indeed have many dedicated arts and education officers, inspectors and advisers in local authorities and arts boards. Writers and academics have clarified the argument and helped to present the case to a wider public. On the way a number of claims have emerged which highlight the significance of involving artists directly in schools and colleges.

Claims made for the work of artists in schools have been documented in several excellent publications over the years such as the Gulbenkian Foundation's pioneering *The Arts in Schools* (1982), the Department of National Heritage's *Setting the Scene* (1996), the Arts Council's *Leading through Learning* (1997), Dick Downing's *Artists in Leeds Schools* (1996), the National Foundation for Educational Research's classic handbook *Artists in Schools* (Sharpe and Dust, 1997) and Sally Manser's *Artists in Residence* (1995). There appears to be, by and large, a consensus in all these accounts regarding key benefits. There are different emphases which reflect different priorities and values; for example, the Leeds document explicitly includes 'challenging the views of the educational institution and its inhabitants' (Downing, 1996: 153) amongst its list of possible purposes of involving artists and media workers in education. The Department of National Heritage and Arts Council comments are, as one would expect, more circumspect.

What follows is a survey of the range of claims made for the work of artists in schools. In the survey the claims are supported with:

- reference, where appropriate, to the relevant sections of the OFSTED *Framework for the Inspection of Schools* (OFSTED, 1995), which are shown in italic print.

- a set of accompanying observations and references highlighting the very wide constellation of interests which acknowledge the relevance and significance of the work of artists in schools.

The general claim is made that the work of artists in schools provides an enhanced learning experience. Artists bring specific experiences, skills and approaches that add to and enrich the work of the teacher in unique ways. The basic categories of maker/presenter of art and teacher/facilitator can then be expanded to include the artist as:

Maker and/or presenter of art

Teacher/facilitator

Teaching resource

Motivator

Role model

Outsider

Broker

(Ofsted Inspection Schedule. 5.3 (Guidance) Cultural development is concerned with both participation in and appreciation of cultural traditions.... Inspectors need to look for evidence of how the school seeks to enrich its pupils' knowledge and experience of their own and other cultural traditions, through the curriculum and through visits, clubs and other activities. Aspects of the curriculum such as history, geography, art, music, dance, drama, literature and the study of language can all contribute positively, for example through opportunities for pupils to:

visit museums and art galleries; work with artists, authors and performers; develop openness towards and value the music and dance of different cultures; appreciate the natural world through art and literature; recognise the contribution of many cultures to mathematics and to scientific and technological development.)

- Watching professional artists at work can provide a special opportunity for students to develop the critical skills needed to evaluate arts activities and processes.[1]

- The arts help us to express our deepest personal and communal thoughts and feelings through the creation of image, metaphor and symbol. Professional artists use the processes of making and presenting art in their daily work. They are therefore primary, living resources and reference points for teaching the arts and developing aesthetic sensitivity and vocabulary.[2]

- For many pupils the artist visiting school is their first encounter with the living world of the arts. A skilled artist in education will structure the experience so that it is specifically appropriate for the target audience or group of participants.

- Professional artists can introduce and access students to aspects of their own cultural traditions in live performance, presentation or workshop process. A live presentation can provide an effective stimulus for critical reflection and discussion on cultural issues.[3]

- The live arts are a vivid way to introduce students to cultural traditions outside their immediate experience, and thereby encourage mutual understanding and a respect for cultural diversity.[4]

- Watching or listening to a performance of a high order can provide a unique 'peak experience' or 'illuminating experience' which is of value in its own right.[5]

Observations

[1]*Artists in Schools* cites an example; '...the education officer of a major opera company described how a group of six year olds had worked with some of the company members on making their own opera. The pupils then visited the company to see a performance of 'A Midsummer Night's Dream'. Their comments afterwards showed that they had a good understanding of the creative processes involved in staging the opera, and had learned the language needed to discuss the performance in some detail' (Sharpe and Dust, 1997: 3).

Observations (continued)

[2]The Gulbenkian report, *The Arts in Schools*, commented: 'We reject the view that the only valid kinds of knowledge are those that are open to deductive reasoning and empirical tests.... The aesthetic, the religious and the moral realms are quite as powerful as those others in conveying knowledge. In our view public education has been too devoted to particular kinds of knowledge at the expense of others which are of equal importance' (Robinson, (ed.), 1982: 24).

[3]In summing up 'The Arts in the Curriculum' conference held by the School Curriculum and Assessment Authority and the Department of National Heritage in February 1997 Dr Nicholas Tate, chief executive of SCAA (now QCA), addressed the vexed issue of cultural heritage and what is meant by it. He observed:

> 'First, that a sense of the worth of one's own culture and a desire to pass it on to the next generation is something we respect....This is not to suggest that passing on cultural traditions is all one is doing in arts education. Nor is it to suggest that pupils should be encouraged to receive these traditions passively, as if they were inheriting the family silver.'

He then pointed out that a respect for one's own cultural traditions did not, and should not, imply an assertion of that culture's superiority over others. Dr Tate added that the arts curriculum should reflect the 'diversity of cultures within our society and the ways in which they have interacted with each other.' He then argued that there is such an abundance of cultural material that choice of subject matter is bound to involve selection and the use of value judgements (SCAA, 1997: 43).

[4]The Arts Council's *Leading through Learning* comments: 'Developments in education and training should be based on a recognition of the benefits that come from mixing different cultural traditions, values and aesthetics to produce new artistic expression, informed by different perspectives and heritage' (ACE, 1997: 6).

[5]*Setting the Scene* has a section titled, 'Why are the arts important?'. One of the reasons given is that: 'At their finest, the arts are pinnacles of human achievement which heighten our sense of humanity, which inspire us, and which are timeless' (DNH, 1996: 2).

In *Towards a Psychology of Being* Abraham Maslow developed the idea of the 'peak experience' in a study of people who seemed to be leading well-adjusted and fulfilling lives. The 'peak experience' could have a discernible and positive impact on attitudes in other contexts (Maslow, 1962).

Rod Taylor describes an 'illuminating experience' as a moment of totally focused attention, of awe. After an initial sensation of inarticulateness, the experience motivates the need to find a language with which to communicate its intensity and reality (Taylor and Andrews, 1993).

The artist as teacher/facilitator

(Ofsted Inspection schedule. 5.1 Teaching. Inspectors must evaluate and report on:

(iii) the extent to which teaching meets the needs of all pupils, paying particular attention to any pupils who have special educational needs or for whom English is an additional language.

Judgements should be based on the extent to which teachers:

employ methods and organisational strategies which match curricular objectives and the needs of all pupils.

See also 5.2 The curriculum and assessment. Inspectors must evaluate and report strengths and weaknesses in: . . . (iv)extra-curricular activities.)

- Artists may provide specialist, professional arts skills not usually available to the classroom teacher. Students may experience these skills in performance, i.e. through responding as audience, or by observing an artist in the process of creating their work.

- Students may develop their own skills through working alongside artists in the presentation or development of a piece of artwork. The artist as co-artist can motivate and encourage students to reach beyond apparent capabilities. Students can learn to appreciate the depth of research, the need to try again, to re-work ideas, to understand the level of commitment and discipline demanded in the creative process.[6]

- Professional artists can provide in-service support and experience for hard-pressed teachers and introduce ways of working that catalyse fresh thinking and approaches.

- Many teachers in schools are artists themselves and the dialogue and working partnership with other practising artists can provide a creative link with the outside world of arts practice. On the other hand, teachers in primary schools need to have skills in an extraordinarily wide range of subject areas and many of them have had little opportunity to train specifically in the arts. Artists of all sorts provide a strong stimulus for teachers in special schools where there is abundant evidence, for example, that working from an aesthetic stimulus provides excellent motivation for language development.[7]

Observations

[6]The NFER *Artists in Schools* cites an example where 'working with a writer had impressed on them (the students) that 'writing is not as easy as you think. You can't just put anything together and think it's finished.' Many of the pupils commented on the process of redrafting that the writer himself went through.... Pupils who had previously found writing 'boring' became motivated to redraft their work several times' (Sharpe and Dust, 1997: 2).

[7]See, for example: Downing, D. and Jones. (1989): *Special Theatre*. Gulbenkian Foundation, and Harland, J. *An Evaluation of a Performing Arts Experiment in a Special School*. Educational Research Vol 32 Number 2 Summer 1990.

(See Inspection Schedule. 5.2. The curriculum and assessment. Inspectors must evaluate and report strengths and weaknesses in: (ii) the provision made for personal and social education, including health education, sex education where appropriate, and attention to drug misuse;

and 5.3. Pupils' spiritual, moral, social and cultural development. Judgements should be based on the extent to which the school provides its pupils with knowledge and insight into values and beliefs and enables them to reflect on their experiences in a way which develops their spiritual awareness and self-knowledge.

See also 5.4. Support, guidance and pupils' welfare. Judgements should be based on the extent to which the school has effective measures to promote discipline and good behaviour and eliminate oppressive behaviour including all forms of harassment and bullying.)

- The work of professional artists may directly relate to an area of study such as a set text, a historical theme or a current moral issue. The artists' input may help to bridge and access areas of knowledge that seem distant from students' immediate experiences.[8]

- Within an arts process children can examine the effects of making decisions. They can create and work in imagined contexts to explore the consequences of making different choices and decisions. The idea of 'role,' for example, enables students to see situations from another perspective, another point of view. This can help to change understanding, challenge prejudices and raise moral awareness. Artists can make a significant contribution to personal, social and spiritual education.[9]

- The example of the artist may encourage creative thought and action and the ability to see new patterns, shapes, ideas and possibilities. The artist's way of thinking is essentially divergent as opposed to convergent, for example a given human problem opens up alternative solutions with a range of possible consequences.[10]

- The professional artist may have a unique contribution to make towards specific aspects of GCSE, A Level or GNVQ courses which qualitatively enhances the teacher's own contribution. Teachers cannot be specialists in all areas of their subjects.[11]

- Artists visiting a school are frequently able to invest greater intensity and energy into a short time than the teacher who needs longer distance rhythm and pacing to work their way through a demanding school day.

Observations

[8]See, for example, in the National Curriculum Interpretations of History, KS1: 'children should be taught to identify different ways in which the past is represented, eg pictures, written accounts, films, television programmes, plays, songs, reproductions of objects, museum displays' (DFE, 1995: History 3). And in KS2: 'children should be taught about the lives of men, women and children at different levels of society in Britain and the ways in which they were affected by changes in industry and transport' (DFE, 1995: History 7).

Observations (continued)

[9]A practical illustration of the above is the work of the National Trust Theatre Company which creates day-long stories and events that take place in significant historical and geographical sites. They involve students directly in imaginatively recreating historical events and building bridges between past and present.

See also QCA Draft guidance (1997) for pilot work on the promotion of pupils' moral development.

For detailed evaluations of theatre programmes targeting health and social issues see: Allen,G. and Dalrymple, L. (1997). *'Forbidden Fire': An Evaluation. An evaluation of a TIE project on autocrime related issues devised and performed by Rent a Role at the Barbican Theatre Plymouth.* University College of St. Mark and St. John, Plymouth. Also Elliston, K. (1994): *Evaluating the Effectiveness of Theatre in Health Education for Sexual Health Education in Schools.* Unpublished dissertation for Master of Science in Health Promotion and Health Education, University of Wales.

[10]*Leading through Learning* makes the following observations: 'Advanced industrial nations increasingly recognise the need for profound change in the way they educate their citizens. The skills and understanding that the arts engender – not least in the use of new information technologies – can make an important contribution to their success, both social and economic.' And again: 'The skills people acquire through studying and practising the arts are those most needed in the modern workplace: communication, co-operation, problem solving, risk taking, flexibility and creativity ... it is estimated that by the year 2000 over 70% of employment will be in the knowledge industries' (ACE, 1997: 5).

In a 1997 RSA lecture, 'The Arts and Industrial Competitiveness' given as part of 'The Arts Matters' series, Sir Alan Cox CBE made the following observations:

'My thesis is that this is an area in which we can use the rich talents of people working in the arts. The arts teach people that they can grow, think for themselves, see ways of using their talents in the workplace directly. People need help and, in the arts, there are talented people who know exactly what creativity is all about. I see the arts as being able to place themselves centrally in this argument. I am not saying the arts provide the only answer, but it is an industry in which enormous creative talent exists and it can play a significant role in helping industry to get to world-class performance' (RSA, 1997: 81).

[11]Sally Manser in *Artists in Residence* gives an example of a secondary school where:

'The Art and Design department has three members of staff all of whom are fine art trained. The GCSE syllabus demands an element of photography and the department is also considering introducing a GNVQ in photography. Staff in the department are keen to extend their skills in photography and suggest inviting a photo-journalist to undertake a residency. The Head of English expresses an interest in the input the artist could make to media studies and a cross-departmental residency is established' (Manser, 1995: 8).

(See Inspection Schedule. 8. English, mathematics and science.

In English, the subject report up to 16 should also draw on evidence of the contribution made by other subjects to pupils' competence in reading, writing, speaking and listening.

See also 4.2. Attitudes, behaviour and personal development. Judgements should be based on the extent to which pupils:

show interest in their work and are willing to sustain concentration and develop their capacity for personal study.

See 4.3. Attendance. Inspectors must evaluate and report on:

pupils' attendance and punctuality, analysing reasons for absence where attendance is poor or where patterns of absence affect particular groups of pupils.)

- Working with an artist in a creative situation encourages concentration, motivation and a predisposition to learn. Motivation is a crucial factor in language development, for example. Emotional identification and empathy with characters within a story, play, opera, dance or painting can trigger a need to know more and encourage deeper learning.[12]

- The vividness of imagery, rhythm, shape and colour of artists' work aids memory recall, even over long periods of time.[13]

- The work of artists can stimulate listening, looking, language and literacy skills and motivate, for example, written work of a high standard. Current research demonstrates a connection between involvement with music and the development of mathematical abilities.[14]

- Working with artists can help to build confidence.

- Working with artists encourages a sense of the joy of learning which generates a positive approach to school life.

- Working with artists can help to identify and explore underlying reasons for poor school attendance and help to engender more positive attitudes to school.[15]

Observations

[12]Jerome Bruner comments: 'What makes the internal sequence of a story even more compelling than the distractions that lie outside it? Are there comparable properties inherent in other activities? Can these be used to train a child to sustain his curiosity beyond the moments's vividness?' (Bruner, 1966: 116)

[13]For reference to a detailed study on the long-term impact of Theatre in Education see: Clark, L. (1984): *Theatre, Memory and Learning. An exposition of the action and the act of a reflexive evaluation.* Unpublished M.A. in Applied Research in Education, East Anglia University.

Observations (continued)

[14]*Leading through Learning* claims that: 'There is growing awareness that children under 5 have great aesthetic learning potential, and evidence that involvement in arts activity before the age of 5 increases overall learning ability' (ACE, 1997: 8). *Setting the Scene* also reports: 'Recent research shows that the arts also help young people in their academic subjects and foster a more positive attitude towards education. For example, new American research suggests that an enhanced music and visual arts curriculum can improve young children's general attitude towards learning and school, and that learning arts skills can encourage mental 'stretching' useful to other curriculum subjects, especially mathematics' (DNH, 1996: 2).

At the SCAA and DNH 'The Arts in the Curriculum' conference in 1997 there were claims from researchers in Rhode Island USA, Norway and Southern Africa that the study of music increased concentration and numeracy skills. However, delegates to the conference were 'very cautious about placing too much emphasis on the consequential learning which can occur from music education, and wished to stress that the raison d'être for music was its own intrinsic value' (SCAA, 1997: 29).

[15]A group of schools in inner city Plymouth received GEST funding to address the problem of truancy. They used the local theatre in education company to explore and open up the issues, across a wide age range, using actors and drama workshop techniques.

The artist as role mode

(See Inspection Schedule 5.2. The curriculum and assessment. Judgements should be based on the extent to which the curriculum: is balanced and broadly based, promotes pupils' intellectual, physical and personal development and prepares pupils for the next stage of education, training or employment.)

(See Inspection schedule 4.2. Attitudes, behaviour and personal development. Inspectors must report on and evaluate pupils' response to the teaching and other provision made by the school, highlighting strengths and weaknesses, as shown by (for example); the quality of relationships in the school, including the degree of racial harmony, where applicable.)

- Students in schools often take a great interest in the 'human' and economic sides of an artist's visit through the questions they raise, for example: How long have you been doing this? Why do you do it? Do you get nervous? Do you get paid? This provides an opportunity to engage in dialogue with an artist and to understand something of the nature of professional commitment and the sheer hard work involved. They can see the artist in the context of 'work' and within a wider social and economic frame.[16]

- Artists from a range of cultural, ethnic, gender and social backgrounds can provide positive, creative role models that can build confidence, break down stereotypes and help a school build up an active Equal Opportunities programme.[17]

The artist as outsider

- Some students may feel able to talk and work more openly with an accepted outsider who is not identified with a teacher role. However, in today's safety conscious environment, in which we have experienced some disturbing events, a school's attitude to the 'stranger' is complex and needs to be handled with respect and sensitivity.

- Through the indirect approach of metaphor and analogy the artist can access difficult and perhaps sensitive areas of understanding.

- Introducing an artist into the teaching frame can enable the teacher to stand back and observe their class at work. The experience can be illuminating for a teacher who may see individual children in a new light.

Observations

[16]*Leading Through Learning* observed that: 'Britain's cultural industries are internationally respected and commercially successful. They directly employ two-thirds of a million people and contribute £6bn a year to Britain's balance of payments' (ACE, 1997: 5).

[17]The activities of AEMS (Arts Education for a Multicultural Society) have already been referred to in chapter two. *Artists in Schools* cites an example where 'a disabled dancer demonstrated that it is possible for someone to achieve in an art form which many people assume is the preserve of the able bodied. His example encouraged disabled children to participate with confidence and enthusiasm' (Sharpe and Dust, 1997: 3).

(See Inspection Schedule 4.2. Attitudes, behaviour and personal development. Inspectors must evaluate and report on pupils' response to the teaching and other provision made by the school, highlighting strengths and weaknesses, as shown by:

the quality of relationships in the school.

other aspects of their personal development, including their contribution to the life of the community.

Judgements should be based on the extent to which pupils:

form constructive relationships with one another, with teachers and other adults, and work collaboratively when required:

show respect for other people's feelings, values and beliefs;

show initiative and are willing to take responsibility.)

- An arts event may enable students from the same or different age groups and key stages to work together and thereby encourage the breaking of barriers and prejudices. The social health of a group or class can have a strong impact on an individual learner's attitudes and achievement.

- The work of the artist may also provide an opportunity for different schools to work and collaborate together. A group of schools, such as an Academic Council or Consortium, may be able to muster more influence in attracting crucial resources for an arts project.

- The presence of artists within the school may help to inspire, encourage and build up a wider creative atmosphere in the school in general. This may be communicated to the wider school community through exhibitions, displays, assemblies and even the 'buzz' from those classes and groups directly involved.

- Visiting artists can help to raise the profile of the arts within the school.[18]

- The artist's work may touch on several areas of the curriculum, help to build bridges between subjects, and thereby encourage cross-curricular thinking and working.

Observations

[18] The Gulbenkian Foundation's *Arts in Schools* comments: 'One effect of vocational pressures in schools is for the arts to be considered as leisure activities, not essential – and not as serious as 'real work'. We have argued against this attitude throughout this report. One way of combating it in schools is for pupils to work with those who have actually made the arts their occupation – to see the commitment and application this involves and demands. This can do much to raise the status of the arts for children and young people' (Robinson, (ed.) 1982: 117).

(See Inspection Schedule. Under 5.5 Partnership with parents and the community. Inspectors must evaluate and report on:

the effectiveness of the school's partnership with parents, highlighting strengths and weaknesses, in terms of: (for example) the contribution which the school's links with the community make to pupils' attainment and personal development.

Also see Inspection Schedule 5.3. Pupils' spiritual, moral, social and cultural development. Judgements should be based on the extent to which the school: . . . encourages pupils to relate positively to others, take responsibility, participate fully in the community, and develop an understanding of citizenship.)

- The presence of an artist can attract curiosity and involvement from parents who may take an increased, active interest in school life.

- Artists can introduce ways of working which may help the nurturing of staff-to-staff and staff-to-student relationships.

- A fruitful scheme with artists may attract positive publicity for the school which could be helpful in promoting a good school image.[19]

- The presence of artists may challenge the institution to consider attitudes and approaches relating to wide areas of school life.

- Skilled community artists can work comfortably in a range of educational and community settings and help to build bridges between school and local community.

- Involvement with artists can help build up the image of a school as a creative focus for a local community. Some schools operate as local arts centres and encourage performances, workshops, exhibitions etcetera on their premises.

- The arts can help pupils to understand and relate to the demands of wider, for example ecological, issues.[20]

Observations

[19]See QCA Draft guidance notes for pilot work: 'The successful promotion of pupils' spiritual, moral and cultural development can:

contribute to success in OFSTED inspections; help to ensure that everyone in the school feels valued as an individual; enhance school success by increasing pupil and teacher motivation'.

[20]See, for example, National Curriculum KS3 Programme of Study for Science: 'Pupils should be given opportunity to:

d. consider the benefits and drawbacks of scientific and technological developments in environmental and other contexts' (DFE, 1995: Science 14).

The NFER handbook *Artists in Schools* (Sharpe and Dust, 1997: 11) describes the range of problems that can arise between school and artists as 'frustrations'. The term is apt. Usually both teachers and artists are aware that their collaboration could be positive for themselves and for the young people involved. But things can go wrong. Eileen Turner of Stirling University refers to 'Tensions at the Interface' (Turner, 1997: 1) between the worlds of the arts and of education. Drawing on these two sources and with reference to our selected projects we can compile our own list of headings:

- artist angst

- teacher tensions

- planning dissonance

- pupil disinterest

- quality versus quantity

- but is it art?

It is important to note that these tensions and problems can be negotiated and worked through.

Artist angst

The tone in which an artist is welcomed into the overall frame of the school can deeply affect how he or she will settle into productive work. Artists do not need to be treated with kid gloves but may need to adjust to the formal rhythm and structure of school life. It can be frustrating when creative momentum, built up through the morning, is summarily brought to a halt because the bell goes or the hall must be made ready for lunch.

Tension may occur when a project is foisted on teachers against their will by an enthusiastic head and without ongoing support and dialogue. Artists have been 'left to it' whilst the teacher retires to the staff room to catch up on marking. In some instances artists have reported feeling they are being used as glorified child minders, let alone supply teachers.

Teacher tensions

Some artists appear to be intolerant and uninformed about teachers' priorities. Teachers have to balance the demands of the curriculum, the needs of their children and the necessity to plan within the realities of the school context. Some artists may, at worst, be blatantly arrogant in their disregard for such priorities.

Some teachers are themselves highly competent artists and may feel uneasy or even threatened by the introduction of another artist into school. Especially so if the artist works in a different way or appears to contradict the teacher's priorities or 'rules'. It is important that teachers consider an artist's visit or residency to be supportive of their role and status in the school. If they feel undermined the impact of any useful work will be frittered away.

Planning dissonance

Sometimes teachers and artists have a different understanding of the intentions of a project. This may occur when a different member of staff, either head or other authority role, negotiates the visit without involving directly the teachers who will be conducting the project at classroom level. The teacher may be enthusiastic about the idea, but feels confused, and perhaps embarrassed by ignorance of what is happening. On the other hand, similar confusion can arise when one member of an arts organisation negotiates the project but another person or group carries it out.

Teachers are having to plan their work a long time ahead and may find, for example, the introduction of a performance by the head, at short notice, difficult to integrate effectively into their ongoing work. On the other hand, funding for artists' projects is sometimes unpredictable and artists have to be opportunists to keep their financial head above water.

Pupil disinterest

Sometimes pupils can feel uninformed about what is happening to the extent that they generate hostility to the project. Pupils are the primary focus of a project and need to feel integrated into and informed about what is going on.

Quantity versus quality

This arises in response to the limited resources available and raises questions as to how widely the jam should be spread or, in the words of Ross and Kamba, do we opt for an 'entitlement for all or a privilege for the few?' (Ross and Kamba, 1997). Several high-quality arts experiences are targeted at small groups of students and therefore are relatively expensive. Turner raises the question: 'As an alternative approach, should we perhaps try to establish what a minimum entitlement for all children in terms of arts experiences should be and cost those as a starting point?' (Turner, 1997: 8).

But is it art?

There is an ongoing, and perhaps necessary, tension between those who see the arts as major experiences in themselves and those who see them as a resource for teaching other areas of the curriculum.

The claims for benefits arising from the work of artists in schools are well documented. The idea of the artist working in schools as maker, presenter and teacher/facilitator can be expanded to include the artist as teaching resource, as motivator, as role model, as outsider and as broker.

The claims are supported by observations and comments by a wide range of people in the arts, in schools, colleges, universities, industry, politics, agencies such as health authorities, prominent foundations and bodies such as QCA and the RSA.

Evidence from teachers, artists, children and parents involved in the selected projects indicates that the claims are being met in practice. The issue of artists helping to raise the level of self-esteem for pupil, teacher and school was a recurrent theme in the interviews.

Input from artists can enhance a school's ability to meet the demands of the Inspection Schedule as outlined in the OFSTED *Framework*. The *Framework* indicates, for example, that inspectors should make judgements as to how the school promotes spiritual, moral and cultural development, the teaching of reading and writing, pupil motivation and positive attitudes to such issues as drugs, bullying and racism.

Problems and tensions arise at 'the interface' between art and education. The problems are surveyed under such headings as artist angst, teacher tensions, planning, quality versus quantity, but is it art? and pupil disinterest. However, most problems can be worked through with good communication and planning.

4 Projects in Practice

Chapter four illustrates the claims made for the work of artists in schools with reference to seven projects in a range of art forms. A description of each project is followed by comments and observations from teachers, artists, children and others involved in the project. A project summary then comments on the outcome of each project and sums up the benefits and problems encountered. Some of the key features that make for a successful, or unsuccessful, outcome are then summarised with reference to all seven projects.

Project one: Speak what we feel

Description of project

Our journey begins in the north, in a large industrial city with a regional theatre that has a long track record of working with schools. The director of the theatre's schools' company is one of the country's most experienced and respected educational theatre practitioners. She had recently come to the view that the language in a current touring production was too complex for children with special needs and so had not included special schools in the publicity mail-out. She was therefore surprised when a teacher contacted her and insisted that his special needs children, with moderate learning difficulties, should not be excluded and promptly invited the company to his school.

The school has approximately 120 pupils, aged 11-19, with a wide range of learning and behavioural difficulty. There are a significant number of pupils who demonstrate unpredictable extremes of behaviour. The performance at the school was, according to theatre director and teacher, highly successful. Despite the complexity of the language the children responded positively and were fully engaged and focused as an audience. Some of the company were experienced theatre in education actors and could integrate the children's impromptu interventions into the show. Afterwards the pupils, fired by the experience, persuaded their teacher to help them create a follow-up drama based on their responses. They invited the director to come and see it. To their surprise she did and proposed that school and company could work together on a project.

The school was without a headteacher at the time and the deputy head encouraged the teacher to begin talks with the theatre company and to perhaps consider a TEC (Training and Enterprise Council) placement scheme. The project hatched eventually by director and teacher was far more ambitious. The theatre invited the teacher to take a one day a week placement with them over a whole year. The placement would culminate in a specially prepared theatre production involving professional director, actors, writer and musician working in collaboration with children and staff of the school and touring to mainstream schools.

The deputy head was well aware that the stumbling block was financial. Some funding was available through the drama adviser and the city's artists-in-schools programme. This would be a very useful contribution but would not cover the cost of the teacher's placement at the theatre. However, she rang the newly appointed head and, after a lengthy discussion, they agreed what for them was a novel way forward. The head and deputy would plan the timetable so that they themselves could cover the teacher's classes when he was out of school. The core group involved in the project would be the dozen pupils, of year 10 and upwards, who had been instrumental in its inception.

The new head thought deeply about the implications. Raising standards of literacy was his core curriculum aim and he was convinced that the creative arts were a basic means to this end. He knew that many of the pupils had real frustrations in articulating their feelings and that the arts, which are effective vehicles for language development, could play an important role in addressing this issue.

The school had been without a head for nearly two years and, according to staff, had experienced a period of instability and demoralisation. The creative arts could play a significant role in raising morale, motivation and the level of expectation throughout the school. The teacher's placement in a professional arts organisation could be immensely valuable as in-service training and in building up a 'collegiate' management approach to the development of the arts within the school.

The regional theatre was staging a version of 'King Lear' at the time. Theatre director and teacher decided to take the line 'Speak what we feel, not what we ought to say' as a starting point. Images from the storm in the play would also act as a stimulus for debate and discussion. Working over several weeks with professional writer, director and actors on material generated by themselves through improvisation and discussion was an intensely powerful experience for the children. The company of actors, director, pupils and teacher explored issues of filial ingratitude, parental love and sibling rivalry. The writer was, in the words of the teacher, 'writing about the pupils' inner turmoil, fears and hopes' and they were being treated as artists themselves in the process. The growth of the participating pupils' self-esteem and confidence was observed by staff throughout the school.

The seventy-minute production, with a cast of twenty (twelve pupils, five professionals and three teachers) opened with a preview at the regional theatre. The audience included teachers of the mainstream and special schools to which it would tour over the following two weeks. On tour there was a morning long workshop process, involving special and mainstream school pupils working together, followed by a presentation of the play in the afternoon.

Taking an official regional theatre production, with a mixed cast of professionals, teachers and young people, on tour to mainstream schools and other venues, was an unpredictable venture for the professional actors. But it transformed the way teachers and children in those schools saw special needs youngsters. The experience touched a lot of people very deeply. Indeed, as one teacher commented about the pupils involved, 'they walked where they may have feared to tread'.

Observations on the project from participants and others

'Working with a professional director and writer who were taking the pupils' ideas and experiences and translating them into the language of drama with them was a profound experience. Likewise when they came to rehearsals the pupils first watched the director directing professional actors who were embodying their (the pupils') inner turmoil. Then in turn they were directed in the same professional way, and with the same respect shown the actors. They all became part of a team. They began to understand the language of theatre in ways in which I couldn't touch in my daily classroom teaching.' *Teacher.*

'By working alongside them we all appreciated what it means to be a professional actor. I myself had really no idea of how demanding it is. Special needs kids have a stigma attached to them, they have low esteem, but the dedication of the actors raised them above this and they were visibly overjoyed at themselves.' *Special Needs Assistant.*

'Although it was exhausting it was a real booster for staff and children. Everyone depended on each other and communication brought people closer together. It was a very moving experience and it really affected relationships in the school.' *Special Needs Assistant.*

'Segregated children being seen as 'experts', breaking barriers and touring a professional show into mainstream schools was a major step up for the school's image.' *Teacher.*

'His (the teacher's) greatest contribution has been to show how successful work can grow from within the special school community and how much can be achieved through initiating work with other agencies.' *Times Educational Supplement, 4192, November 1996, IX.*

Tensions

'The show was billed as a professional one. We needed at times to point out that the project was difficult for artists as well as children. As professionals they would be working alongside youngsters whose behaviour could be dramatically unpredictable. It was risky for them professionally.' *Artist.*

'We set off to use the kids more in performance but cut back on the writing and working process as a response to the pressures of time. We dropped some atmospheric scenes with the pupils in order to clarify the story. Artistic discipline sometimes made demands contrary to my perception of the educational needs of children at that moment; 'something has to go, we'll not use the kids here'.' *Teacher.*

Summary of project

This was an ambitious project which made huge demands on both staff and children involved. The project grew out of an extensive process of dialogue between theatre and school which was given positive encouragement by the head and deputy head. The working relationship between arts organisation and school was open-ended and the theatre went out of its way to respond to the needs of the school.

Detailed planning was integrated into the teacher's placement at the theatre, which meant that the process of planning was thorough and was given adequate time. Generous investment of time, personnel and resources from the regional theatre, the support of the local authority drama adviser and a contribution from the city's artists-in-schools programme gave the project a sound foundation. There was one point of tension during the planning when, according to the head, the project became too demanding and had to be 'reined in'.

The preparation and rehearsal period was a unique opportunity for children and staff to gain first-hand understanding of the degree of commitment, teamwork and creativity required in the devising, writing and rehearsal of a 'professional' theatre production. According to staff and pupils, working with professional artists raised pupils' expectations and enabled them to achieve high standards of performance and ensemble work.

Observations, from staff, of children's behaviour and attitudes from before and after the project showed that the experience raised the self-esteem and confidence of the pupils involved. Positive attitudes were carried over into the classroom and were reflected in the quality of pupils' spoken and written language work.

According to teachers from the mainstream schools visited by the production, the project successfully changed the stereotypical attitudes of their pupils to special needs children. It is not yet clear how successful the project has been in generating a collaborative approach to creative arts teaching in the school.

'Speak what we feel' involved a relatively large investment of resources targeted initially at a small number of pupils. The expense was justifiable on account of the real depth of experience given to the children involved and the teacher on placement, the raising of morale and esteem throughout the school and the impact of the production on mainstream schools during and following an exhausting two-week tour.

Project two: Two continents

Description of project

And so further west, to another industrial city and a trilingual Asian artist whose own prints and paintings have been inspired by the patterns and colours of Phulkaris, translated as 'flower work'. The ability to move easily between different modes of expression is a real asset for this British woman artist who is deeply proud of her Sikh and Punjabi affiliations. Some time ago the artist had worked successfully on an art and language project with a group of inner city schools. The intention of this project had been to develop the English language skills of bilingual children through encounter with original works of art. The education officer of the local gallery had played a key co-ordinating role in initiating the project and invited the artist, whose own work was exhibited in the gallery, to develop her relationship with one school in particular.

The school concerned is an inner city school with a large percentage of Asian children who engage with two cultures and languages in their daily lives. The school has an arts policy and, according to the arts co-ordinator, 'regularly invites practising artists into our school.' The head is concerned about the low self-esteem of many of her children. Many of the parents are not literate, certainly in English, and English is a second language for a majority of her pupils. There is a need for imagination and creativity to help the children access core curriculum skills and raise the level of confidence and achievement. The colourful displays around the school of paintings and artefacts from diverse cultural backgrounds provide a rich and encouraging environment in which to address this need.

The project related directly to several components of the National Curriculum Key Stage One Programme of Study for Art, and the school arts co-ordinator was keen to use the artist's extensive experience, as artist and teacher, to help her colleagues gain skills and confidence in their own art teaching. In collaboration with the gallery the school has designed a programme of study to coincide with exhibitions and artists' availability for workshop and discussion. The gallery also produces an educational CD-Rom featuring 70 Western and non-Western works of art from the collections of the city art galleries and museums, including work from the project artist.

The new initiative would involve the artist painting a large floor cloth exploring the theme of travel between two continents, both today and in Tudor and Moghul times. The gallery made an application to the Arts Council to support the project but was unsuccessful. However, education officer and school managed to obtain resources from the LEA which were then matched by the regional arts board (RAB).

A classroom space was set aside for the residency and the head supported the artist's insistence that the children should use high-quality painting materials. Time was included in the planning process for the artist to transform a classroom into a studio and organise the space and materials as she saw fit. The residency had a planning stage over several weeks, one setting up day and six days to complete the painting.

During this time the school had been working with the local health authority on a community project concerned with health hazards arising from travel overseas. There was a possibility that resources would be available to employ a dancer for this project. It became apparent that the two projects could unite and that the visual artist and the dancer could collaborate to bring the two strands together. The images of the two continents created by artist and children would then be given further life and form in the dance.

Before they started painting the artist showed the children lots of pictures from both cultures to help them get a feel for the similarities and differences. The large floor mat had been divided into two halves representing two worlds. One half represented ideas about Tudor England the other half represented aspects and moods of Moghul life. In one of the early dance workshops the children had been working on traditional Bhartanatym movement, and the artist used the children's feet and hand positions as a starting point for their paintwork.

During the residency specific skills, such as drawing, stencil work and printing techniques, were used extensively and communicated widely throughout the school. In the process staff became, in the words of the arts co-ordinator, more confident about their own art teaching.

The project created a buzz of excitement in the school and local community. Although one class would work with the artist to paint the map, other classes would come to see, in some instances, their brothers and sisters at work. Parents were also invited and the head's commitment to the idea of family pervading the school ethos meant that many did come. Whilst work was in progress, the gallery education officer also organised an in-service course at the school, focusing on the project, which was attended by over forty artists, teachers and students.

The health, education and community strands of the project were drawn together at a public presentation evening, which was well attended by an enthusiastic audience of parents, children, education and health officers and civic dignitaries. Recollecting the experience, some weeks later on a cold railway platform in southern England, the artist recalled warmly the energy of the children's enthusiasm, the richness of their imagination and the motivating encouragement and support of the headteacher.

Observations on the project from participants and others

'The children worked incredibly hard with the artist. They learnt how much hard work goes into a project like this. They were able to achieve such good results because the artist was right there working together with them and constantly encouraging them; it was 'their' painting.' *Teacher.*

'A teachers' inset course visited the studio space when the artist was setting up. This gave them a real insight into the kind of preparation needed to make good use of an artist in residence. The same teachers had an opportunity to visit the project on the Open Studio session which was held towards the end of the residency. This was a real success; the school's warm welcoming atmosphere was extended to forty teachers and artists.' *Project evaluation, gallery education officer.*

'Discussing and working with an artist highlighted the value of using living artists and original works of art to stimulate language and art work.' *LEA report.*

'The painted dance floor by the children and the artist turned out to be a truly wonderful thing. The fairly complex idea which involved linking the history of two continents (the Tudors and Moghuls) through maps and travel to health issues involved in travelling today was really taken on board by the children and artists and influenced and inspired this new piece of art work.' *Project evaluation, gallery education officer.*

'The project gave the children and the school a sense of pride and achievement. I can show you one child who was considered to be dreamy and unfocused but was transformed during the project, becoming a different person. Another child was very clumsy but through the painting and the dance came to have what we could only call a sense of grace.' *Home–school liaison officer.*

'The artist helped the children to make sense of their experience of having roots and families in very different countries, with very different cultures, thousands of miles apart.' *Teacher.*

Tensions

'The theoretical content of the project was very demanding. We were trying to bring in the movements already improvised in the dance, travelling, maps, health issues and school curriculum with Moghuls and Tudors. We should have narrowed down on the content and dealt with a few selected themes more profoundly.' *Artist.*

'It would have been helpful to have had planning time during the residency for artists and teachers to discuss progress without the children being present. Also, there was not enough time for the visual artist to discuss and talk about her own work.' *Gallery education officer.*

'It was late in the day when we realised how the health/dance project could collaborate with the visual arts project. As a result they emerged as two separate strands rather than one organic project.' *Artist.*

Summary of project

This colourful and imaginative project grew out of a previous art and literacy programme with the same artist. The project was well planned and organised between the head and arts co-ordinator at the school, the local gallery education officer and the artist. An appropriate space was made available and time was included in the planning for the artist to adapt the space to her needs. The use of good-quality paint and materials encouraged a positive attitude from the children at the beginning of the project. In the artist's view the consistent support of the head was crucial in the planning and delivery of the project.

As the project gathered momentum, and the links with the health project were established, more ideas were taken on board than could realistically be explored and developed over one week. However, the finished floor cloth painting was rich in colour and detail and visually very impressive.

Participating children were totally absorbed in the painting process and learnt a great deal about the creation of an ambitious project from conception to completion. Over a year later individual children were still keen to point out the details of the floor cloth that they had themselves designed, drawn and painted. The project had given the pupils, and the school, a sense of pride and achievement.

The artist was able to speak in three languages. As they were all working together on the floor cloth she could move between languages, extending vocabulary, drawing comparisons and really making the most of the children's complete absorption in the painting.

The project helped staff at the school to gain greater confidence in their own art teaching, especially in the areas of stencil work and printing techniques. The in-service session, focusing on the project, was well attended by artists, teachers and students. This was arranged by the gallery education officer as part of a strategy to maximise the impact of artist residencies and to disseminate good practice.

The gallery education officer and school arts co-ordinator produced an accessible evaluation form for school, artist and gallery to complete. The project has led to increased co-operation between gallery and school in the planning of the art curriculum and the place of visiting artists within it.

Project three: Yes, we feel like composers

Description of project

The train draws into the capital. A young composer and orchestral education officer recollect the progress of a unique music project spanning three years. An arts venue, with a national focus and significance, had negotiated a music project with six inner city schools which involved one class from each school. The classes were in year 7, and participated in the project till the end of year 9.

The project had been conceived by the education department of the arts venue working in collaboration with the local University's Institute of Education. The Institute would evaluate the ongoing project over the three years. One aim was to encourage pupils to develop a depth of musical understanding which would enable them to make informed choices as to whether they continued their music studies at year 10. A second aim was to bring teachers, pupils and a wide range of high calibre professional musicians together to make and share music. The third aim was to provide an opportunity to explore, in depth, a wide range of musical activities from diverse cultural backgrounds.

One of the schools involved had been invited to participate following the withdrawal of another school. 'This is one of the poorest boroughs in the country, most of these children would never consider going to a theatre or concert,' said the headteacher, 'so when an opportunity like this comes along I grab it and work out how we'll do it afterwards. Enrichment of the curriculum is a high priority for us.' The head's policy of quick response to such opportunities is based on her belief in the link between the growth of the arts in the school over the past four years and the raising of overall academic achievement in the same period. It is a self-evident proposition to her that if children are motivated and confident they are more likely to learn and achieve in all areas. The arts are powerful, and necessary, tools to this end.

Integrating a major three-year project into the school timetable, at short notice, was a challenging operation. It was made possible through the determination of the head, the enthusiasm of the head of music and the co-operation of the staff. Constraints of timetabling governed the choice of which class could participate though, as it turned out, the class chosen was genuinely representative of ability range and cultural diversity across the year group.

Over three years the children worked closely with a range of composers and musicians of different cultures and styles. In the first year they learnt to play the gamelan and had a series of workshops transferring gamelan techniques onto classroom instruments. They then composed their own pieces inspired by the sounds and structures of gamelan music. They attended rehearsals at the arts venue for an important new composition and interviewed the composer. With help from other musicians the pupils then studied the style of the composer and created their own compositions, based on this style, which were later performed at the centre. In the second year the children had the opportunity to explore rhythms and percussion from around the world in workshops with a range of high-profile international musicians. They were then involved, with other schools, in a performance of Samba, Clave and West African music at the arts venue. Some of the pupils then worked with a well-known British composer to create a new piece which was included in a professional public concert at the venue. They interviewed prominent film composers and, again with help from other musicians, created their own sound tracks. Each school chose a film clip ranging from an extract from a disaster movie to a car advert, as their stimulus. In the third year visiting musicians worked on new rhythms with the pupils, helped them put together their own band and write their own music and then rehearsed the pupils in readiness for a final concert at the venue.

Talking to the children a year after the project's completion showed that the experience had shifted their perceptions of and attitudes to music. For example, one pupil was able to describe how, since taking part in the project, she had been more aware of the nature and rhythm of sounds in the street, the home or the playground; the project had taught her to listen with awareness and sensitivity.

Composer and teacher both recollected the real problems they had encountered. Communication between venue and school was sometimes unclear. It is difficult for a school to respond flexibly to last-minute initiatives and some of the less experienced musicians could not understand the teachers' preoccupation with such mundane issues as toilets, buses and getting to the next lesson on time. But all agreed that it was a rich and positive experience of making, performing and listening to music that children and teachers would never forget.

Observation on the project from participants and others

'Their (the children's) recorded compositions show quite high levels of musical thinking and the clear musical influence of the various projects.' *Institute of Education evaluation.*

'As a composer I am used to dealing with musical material daily and learning what will work well and how musical ideas can be progressed and developed. The classroom teacher has not time to dedicate to composition in the same way. In this instance I could keep the children artistically focused on an idea and make connections between their own work and that of the composer involved. Then for the children to interview the composer, watch him rehearse and perform with professionals deepened the links and their musical understanding.' *Artist.*

'One of the aims of the project was to encourage enthusiasm for and understanding of music so that the pupils could make informed choices about opting for music in year ten. The project was able to fulfil this intention far more successfully than I could do by myself.' *Teacher.*

'When you asked the children about the project I wondered how much they would remember; I worked out that they were talking in detail about something that happened in 1995, three years ago, with what seemed to be a quite clear memory. I was very surprised at how much they had retained, and in such detail.' *Teacher.*

'I still watch TV differently after working with that composer because I'm thinking about how they're using the music to make you have certain feelings. I'd never thought about it before.' *Pupil, recalling a project after eighteen months.*

'The children had these opportunities to ask prominent musicians and composers about their work and their straightforward and direct questions such as, do you get paid for it? were refreshing and honest.' *Teacher.*

'There was a female percussionist who was a very strong role model for the girls. She came across as skilled, demanding high standards from herself and the children, and a decisive group leader.' *Artist.*

'Staff observed that this was the year 9 class that had gelled over the three years. The group contained a wide range of ability and social and cultural background. It was observed that they seemed unusually able to embrace diversity and displayed a sense of being part of a team and a higher degree of open-mindedness than their peers in other classes.' *Teacher. (Endorsed by Institute of Education evaluation.)*

Tensions

'It is harder to get artists in for longer periods of time but we need to in order to establish trust and allow opportunity to develop ideas and go with the flow of children's creativity. It is not the same as a normal music lesson. The inflexibility of the timetable makes this difficult. For example, you have a session in the morning, then you can't see the next group for a couple of hours because of timetabling restrictions. The orchestra is paying for musicians just to wait around.' *Artist.*

'Teachers have to think instinctively of toilets, lunch, buses, being on time for the next lesson. Some of the less experienced artists were not willing to accommodate their thinking to these seemingly trivial problems.' *Teacher.*

'The process led to a re-evaluation of my teaching practice. People were referring to professional musicians coming into the school. But I am a professional musician too. How can the teacher as artist in their own right be acknowledged? What is really going on is that other artists are coming into school to enhance the work of artists who are already there.' *Teacher.*

Summary of project

The project was initiated by a prestigious arts venue in collaboration with the local University's Institute of Education. When one of the schools dropped out of the project the organisers invited this inner city girls' school to participate. The invitation was at short notice but the head, in collaboration with the head of music, made the decision to go ahead. The decision was in line with the head's commitment to provide wide cultural opportunities for children at the school.

Preliminary planning for the project had already taken place. Fitting an ambitious and demanding project into the school timetable put pressure on staff and pupils. Clear and firm leadership from the head enabled the project to proceed. There were planning and organisational problems throughout the project which were largely attributed to unclear communication between arts venue and school. Some of the less experienced musicians found it difficult to understand the practical priorities of teachers and the inevitable constraints of working in an educational institution.

The project was a rich musical experience for pupils which, over the course of three years, related directly to many areas of the Key Stage 3 National Curriculum for Music in relation to performing and composing, listening and appraising. Talking to children who had been involved confirmed the positive impact on them. Their recall of events, workshops and interviews that had taken place three years ago was impressive.

Pupils gained direct experience of composing and performing with a wide range of musicians from diverse cultural backgrounds. They learnt much about teamwork, professional discipline and the need to work and re-work ideas in order to reach high standards. Working with well-known musicians at a prestigious arts venue gave pupils confidence and helped to challenge preconceptions, and fears, about such venues. The project was a major in-service opportunity for the head of music and the experience increased her confidence and enthusiasm and enhanced her own skills, especially in the area of composition.

It was an important feature of the project that the local University's Institute of Education had undertaken to evaluate the project over the three years. Their evaluation confirmed that the children had developed 'a real depth of musical understanding' and that the teacher experienced an enhancement of her own skills and enthusiasm. The evaluation also confirmed other staff's observations that this class, although it started with the same range of cultural, academic and social diversity as the others, had been the one class in that year group to maintain a sense of 'homogeneity' over the three years.

Providing a rich experience of this nature over three years is inevitably expensive. In this instance the expense was justifiable on the grounds that there were extensive and ongoing benefits for pupils and teachers in all the six schools involved. The Institute of Education evaluation demonstrated the rich potential of such projects in both academic and social terms.

The project was a unique in-service opportunity for the head of music to carry over the experience into the wider music curriculum; an opportunity that has been firmly grasped to the benefit of many pupils, and staff, throughout the school. A recent OFSTED inspection showed that the standard of music teaching in the school was very high.

Description of project

Over a cup of coffee in the rehearsal room of a northern based dance company a young black dancer described a residency he had undertaken some months previously. The residency took place in a school three hundred miles away south of the capital. He had worked in the school before and was supportive of the dance teacher's unswerving commitment to the development of dance in the school and local community. The teacher, with the full support of the head, had responded to an imaginative proposal from the district council.

The district council had invited applications from local organisations to create maps of the area in a range of forms. The dance teacher had proposed that the school develop links already established with the dance company, and this particular dancer, to create a map through movement. The proposal was accepted and the council awarded the school a grant to pay the dancer's fees. The headteacher and the head of dance recognised that the project would be a unique opportunity for the dance students to work in real depth with a skilled professional. The project would also fit in with the school's annual arts festival and help build up the school's profile as a potential community arts centre.

The residency would involve several visits from the dancer over four months culminating in a final, focused rehearsal period before public presentation. In June the dancer visited the school to meet the pupils involved and to set preparatory tasks for both them and the teacher. In July the dancer returned to carry out an intensive programme of workshops. The main residency visits took place throughout September and October leading to the performance at the end of October. The performance would be part of the wider arts festival that has become an annual event for school and community. The deputy head was keen to be supportive and she took groups of children on 'field trips' to research the local area. They gathered information, took photographs of contrasting neighbourhoods, interviewed people of all ages and collated the material as the springboard for devising the dance.

The participants had been chosen by the dancer, through audition, during his visit in June. Those unsuccessful for this production would re-work a previous dance presentation for the festival with the teacher. This meant that teacher and dancer would not be able to work practically together, as they had hoped, but that everybody who wished to be could be involved in some way.

The dance explored features of the local area in four sections. The first section portrayed, with considerable humour, the diversity and types of people who lived locally or who came in from outside. The second section was a more fluid representation of the pleasant surrounding countryside and immediate environment. The third was an energetic expression of the significance and impact of the nearby racing circuit and motorway on local communities, and the fourth section explored and celebrated the experience of being young in that locality.

The dancer is highly respected in the dance world for his technical expertise, choreographic skills and physical discipline. To translate their written and recorded research material into movement and image was a highly demanding task for the group and the dancer demanded high standards. The rehearsal process was also technically and imaginatively very demanding and some of the students found it hard to keep pace with the momentum.

During the devising process with the dancer it became apparent that, in order to express the significance of the nearby motorway and racing circuit, some of the dance could usefully be 'on wheels.' A group of older boys, who were very skilful skaters, began to watch rehearsals from the doorway, hinting that the dancers would benefit from some professional advice. The dancer, to the initial consternation of the teachers, invited them to participate. Although it was at a late stage of rehearsal and time was at a premium, the boys accepted the dancer's challenge and became part of the team. The practical contribution of the boys was, in the words of one participant, 'somewhere between dance and skating', but their genuinely committed involvement and positive attitude to the ritual and discipline of rehearsal were widely recognised throughout the school.

As with many good projects there were tensions in the delivery. The dancer wanted the work to be of a high standard and put pressure on the dance teacher and head to get children released from classes at the later stages of rehearsal. But teachers in other subjects are also concerned about their own standards and priorities and increasingly find it difficult to acquiesce easily to such demands. By the time of the festival the teacher was exhausted and unwell, which meant she had no time to evaluate the project as she had intended. However, there was no doubt that the project had a strong impact on both participants and audience. So much so that the school was being asked to tour the production to other schools for months after the festival performance.

The dancer was an inspirational role model for both girls and boys. The dance group recognised and respected his impressive choreographic and dance skills. His athletic physicality and discipline, positive attitude and a sharp wit made him acceptable and 'cool' in the boys' eyes and radically shifted their perception of dance.

Observations on the project from participants and others

'The pupils went on field trips to the railway stations in the area to contrast different social settings, they took photographs of the surrounding countryside, they observed the impact of the nearby motorways and the motor racing circuit on the pace and quality of life, they discussed and shared their own and others' feelings about being a young person in the area. They then had to present all this to the dancer and explore it in gesture, movement, sound and rhythm in order to make their maps become a living reality. It was a very creative proposal and challenge from the district council.' *Teacher*.

'The dancer was really great and inspiring when he was with us. We then had to do a lot of rehearsing by ourselves to get it right. That was really hard work and we used to argue quite a lot. It was really frustrating when we had agreed to practise at a certain time and someone didn't turn up.' *Pupil*.

'It gave me commitment to come to school. There was something to look forward to. It wasn't like you wake up and you think, 'oh, school again', I actually wanted to come to school. That dancer inspired you to get interested.' *Pupil*.

'Other pupils were fascinated by the effect the dancer was having on the dance group and how he had drawn in the boys to participate. There was an expectancy in the air and a lot of people were desperately keen to see the outcome.' *Head*.

'We have a policy to introduce artists into school in order to enrich and extend the pupils' experiences. We are also aware of how this helps us to develop the school's links with the local community. This is why we have developed the festival idea. In turn this has given us a foundation to apply, successfully, for a Lottery feasibility study in order to create an arts centre on the site for use between school and community.' *Head*.

Tensions

'As we approached the performance itself the dancer, understandably, wanted more time to rehearse. This put pressure on colleagues who, understandably, did not wish the pupils to miss important lessons. There was quite a bit of tension.' *Teacher*.

'My responsibility for the wider festival meant that we couldn't work together as hoped. I was aware that, although the dancer was very talented, he had not been trained to teach. He could inspire the pupils with an idea but some of them could not get there. As a teacher who knows the youngsters I would have been able to help here. Likewise I was not able to capitalise on his performance and choreographic skills as much as I would have liked. We were all disappointed that he could not be involved in follow-up and progression sessions.' *Teacher*.

Summary of project

'Maps alive' arose from the head of dance's imaginative response to an initiative from the district council. The planning for the project took place over the summer term and this enabled maximum benefit to be gained from the autumn residency. In responding to the interest shown by many pupils in the wider festival the teacher decided to work on an additional dance project herself. This meant that teacher and dancer could not practically work together as originally hoped. A significant in-service opportunity for the teacher (and the dancer) was, to some extent, lost.

The extensive research undertaken by the pupils, with the help of the deputy head, meant that the pupils felt a sense of ownership of the project. They saw their own ideas being used directly in the process of choreography. The pupils learnt a great deal about the creation of an original dance piece from initial idea to final form and performance. According to the head of dance the dancer was technically very demanding, insisted on high standards and pushed the dancers to the limits of their abilities and understanding. In the teacher's view some of the pupils could have 'gone further' if she herself had been able to attend more rehearsals and act as mediator and communicator between dancer and pupils.

The decision, at a late stage, to involve the group of boys for the roller blading sequence bore fruit. Although their understanding of dance was limited they made a genuine contribution to the project. The personality of the dancer was the key factor in encouraging their motivation, focus and discipline during demanding rehearsals. Boys and girls worked collaboratively and supportively, much to the surprise of several members of staff.

As the performance date came closer there were tensions arising from the dancer's requests for more rehearsals during school time. The tensions were resolved with support from the head who, as well as appreciating the unique opportunity afforded the dancers, was also aware of the wider significance of the project for the developing role of the school as a community arts centre.

The high standard of performance achieved was noted by officers from the regional arts board and the district council, and was reflected in the invitations to tour the project to several schools in the region.

The project effectively enhanced the pupils' skills in relation to dance requirements in Key Stage 4 of the dance option within the National Curriculum for Physical Education, especially in relation to the requirement that pupils should be taught: 'to compose and perform, accurately and expressively, increasingly complex and demanding dances that successfully communicate the dancer's intention'. The head of dance commented that, although dancer and teacher had not collaborated as planned, the project had done much to enhance her own choreographic skills and understanding.

Project five: As deep as platform shoes

Description of project

To central England now and a chance to pick up on the work of a talented poet who dedicates the major part of his working life to working with children in schools. An oncoming bout of flu did not detract from his seemingly boundless inventiveness in inspiring children to create images with words and gesture, helping them experience the joy of playing with language and the disciplined satisfaction of crafting images into meaning.

The residency had been set up through a county-wide arts agency which covered most of the costs and involved the poet being resident in a number of schools over several weeks. The intention was for the project to be cross-phase involving a secondary school and several primary schools. Schools would put in bids to participate and would be expected to make a financial contribution. The work itself would consist of a series of workshop activities and rehearsals culminating in a shared performance at the secondary school.

A class teacher in one of the primary schools had persuaded herself to get involved. The school's English SATS results had been average and the staff felt they needed an effective stimulus to spark enthusiasm for written work. The teacher herself lacked confidence in her ability to teach poetry and the head encouraged her to take part in the project. He has historically taken an opportunistic attitude towards having artists visit the school and supports any staff interest on an *ad hoc* basis. There is currently no formal arts policy in place.

The children and teacher had to walk twenty minutes or so to the secondary school to take part in the workshops. This was not a popular move, which also caused some embarrassment to the poet. He felt himself to be in the role of host and yet sometimes found himself sorting out double bookings for the working space or, on a particularly hot day, not being able to offer the primary children a drink after their walk.

Despite the early tensions the teacher soon responded to the poet's love for language and his real talent to draw ideas from the children's own experience. He was a gifted storyteller with the capacity to generate high energy and commitment which he could then focus and develop. The verbal and physical expression of the children's poetry was highly important to him.

At one stage of the residency the pupils, in the words of the poet, 'were looking at ideas of personification and developing images – The Cleaning Crow was taking images all to do with cleaning, and developing a conceit out of this to end up with a powerful result - this poem came out of oral word play, observation, input into a notebook and group editing to come up with a final polished version'.

> The Cleaning Crow
>
> Crow hoovering the air,
> Wearing his crooked apron
> He is a feather duster
> Sweeping across the house of the sky
> He is black like burnt toast,
> Scorched by the chef sun.
> Crow is a dirt devil,
> His wings a dustpan and brush,
> Scooping up a cloud of dust,
> Claws sharp as scouring pads.

Similarly with another poem:

> If I was the wind what would I wear?
>
> Bluey jeans
> & Shoetrees
>
> A wig of clouds
> & A hat of earth
>
> A cool cloud-coat
> With leather (s) leaves
> Crow gloves
> & Cufflink stars.

It was moving to hear a seasoned primary teacher, with several years' classroom experience, speaking with such passion about something she had until recently felt so reticent towards. In her view, endorsed by the head, the project had made a real impact on the children's writing skills and raised her own sights as to the quality of work she could draw from them. Her enthusiasm was communicated to colleagues through the inset work she had planned to enable them share something of her experience. The quality of the children's writing exhibited on the school walls was indeed a credit to teacher, children and poet.

Observations on the project from participants and others

'The poet was enthusiastic about the children's work. He seemed genuinely excited about what they produced. The children felt he was impressed, that he valued them as artists. Then he could put pressure on them to extend themselves. They learnt that to get published you need to work and re-work ideas over and over again. I was also impressed by the sophistication of the language he stimulated from them. I was quite surprised to hear my children talking about alliteration, similes, metaphors and relating these figures of speech confidently to their own writing.' *Teacher.*

'The poet enthused the children – and me. As a teacher I could not possibly sustain that level of energy throughout the day. I could see he was tired by the end of a session, but we were literally inspired by his input.' *Teacher.*

'I can honestly say that this project was a significant life event for my child. He had previously been identified as needing extra help in spelling; he didn't seem to make the connection between words and what they meant. The poet (a male poet too!) was incredibly charismatic and putting the children's ideas into rhythm, sounds and movement really got my son excited with the connections he could make. He's gone into the secondary school now and in terms of his language work it gave him so much confidence. It was a real break-through.' *Parent.*

'This was a new class and as yet I had not had much opportunity to get to know them. In some of the sessions I was able to detach myself watch the class at work with the poet. Watching them work in groups was particularly useful in helping me to quickly work out the social dynamics of the class.' *Teacher.*

Tensions

'A different teacher attended the introductory session with the poet. When we began work I found it difficult to know what my role was. The first session was a bit tense. We also had a twenty-minute walk to the secondary school where the sessions took place. The children and staff would have preferred to work in our own base. Working in the secondary school was really a cross-phase gesture rather than meaningful co-operation. The exception to this was the performance we gave to their year 7's.' *Teacher.*

'The poet wanted to work with a group of fifteen. This would have created huge tensions for me in the school and was just not practical.' *Teacher*.

'A residency should be something special. If I have to work with thirty or more children the exercise becomes something different, less individually and small group focused. It affects the nature and certainly the quality of what I can do. Why else do parents pay huge amounts of money to send their children to schools with classes of fifteen or so?' *Artist*.

Summary of project

This project was initiated by a regional arts education agency which raised the bulk of the resources, negotiated with the poet, devised the overall structure and invited schools to participate.

The participating teacher was unable to attend an initial planning meeting which was attended by one of her colleagues. As a result she did not clearly understand, in detail, what the project would involve. This was reflected in the early sessions with the poet in which she was unclear about her role. The decision to hold the poetry sessions in the secondary school caused tensions for the primary children and teachers involved who had a twenty-minute walk at the beginning and end of each session. In the teacher's view this was a waste of time and put the children in the wrong frame of mind for serious work.

There was a further planning and communication-related problem at the end of the residency when the agency asked the school for its financial contribution. The school had not clearly understood this was part of the contract.

The teacher was eventually very impressed with the poet's range of skills. He worked effectively from the children's own experience to create vivid images. He then had the teaching skills to help children craft their initial images into words and rhythm. The teacher was impressed by the poet's attention to detail and his constant encouragement of the children to work and re-work their ideas to achieve high standards. The poet was also an experienced storyteller, with a flamboyant personality, and he rehearsed the children rigorously and imaginatively to present their work using visual images, sound and movement.

The project was a rich contribution to several Key Stage 2 English requirements, including those that pupils should be taught to plan, draft, revise, proof-read and present their written work and that they should be 'taught to use writing as a means of developing, organising and communicating ideas'.

The teacher was impressed with how the children learnt to talk with confidence and understanding about the sometimes complex figures of speech they were using in their poems.

The high standard of writing displayed throughout the school is a testimony to the ongoing impact of the residency on children and teacher. The teacher herself has gained skills and confidence in her teaching of creative writing and has planned an in-service course to spread her ideas and enthusiasm to colleagues.

Project six: The girl that could be me

Description of project

It seemed the meeting was destined never to take place. Confusion over time and place in the capital, a breakdown on the motorway, roadworks and traffic jams, but eventually managing to arrive in the same foyer at the same regional theatre at the same time!

The writer/director had done a lot of creative work with young people. When she was approached by the theatre in education company to write and direct a play about young women and drugs she had a clear idea of what she did *not* want to do. She did not want to 'preach, condemn or judge.' Fourteen plus year olds are a 'notoriously difficult theatrical audience'. What she did want to do would involve an exhaustive research process with young people, drug and other agencies, libraries, resource centres and clubs, 'where I felt about one hundred and ninety seven!'

Theatre in education has taken a buffeting over the past two decades. The company is one of the few supported by their local authority that has been able to evolve and develop its work. Developing a relationship with key agencies such as the health authority has been central to this process. The company works in close collaboration with the county drugs unit, which provides advice, follow up resources and, in some cases, financial backing.

The production was well resourced and supported. The company consisted of five young women with a range of performance skills and experience of the issues. There were three main performers, one musician who could be both disc jockey and character, and a stage manager who could also act. The play showed five very different characters who represented a wide range of attitude towards drugs issues.

Following the writer's extensive research process a working script was produced and discussed with the theatre company's management and the drugs unit. Follow-up material for classroom use was devised by the drugs unit. This would link characters, and the choices they faced and made, with important information and background. The intention was that young people would be well informed and confident enough to make autonomous choices that were in their own interest. Writer/director and actors would then have a further five weeks to rehearse the final production before embarking on a long and arduous tour.

The play toured widely to schools in the area. One of the schools it visited was situated in one of the largest council estates in Europe. The drama teacher here had huge respect for his local company and used them whenever possible: 'I know their work is of a high standard and, after all, it's our service, we pay for it!' He worked closely on this occasion with the PSS (Personal and Social Skills) and English departments. Unfortunately the detailed follow-up resources could not be used to the full as the availability of the play did not coincide with the drugs education module in a complex PSS timetable. The drama teacher appreciates the pressure put on colleagues by events that disrupt the timetable especially, as on this occasion, when year 10 and year 11 pupils are involved. However, he had confidence in the company and was convinced that this was an important experience and opportunity for both pupils and staff. The theatre company and drugs unit provided a detailed follow-up package for classroom use. Realising the constraints of the timetable the drama teacher provided a more accessible precis of the material for colleagues.

On this occasion the company had decided to trust the power of a strong piece of theatre to engage young people with the issues. There was no workshop process with the actors following the show. The company invested their energies in creating a high-quality piece of theatre that was strikingly visual and incorporated 'up to the minute music' that was recognisable and accessible to the audience. It was be a short, vivid 'bungee jump' of an experience that challenged, disturbed and promoted deep thinking. Talking eighteen months later to young people who had seen the production confirmed the achievement of the company's aim. The pupils' detailed recollection of the characters, incidents and dilemmas in the play showed that it had made a strong impact.

Encouraging staff to contribute to the vision of the school is an important element of the head's management philosophy. A sense of being part of a team is generated when colleagues can suggest 'what about...?' or 'could I try...?'. Visits from artists are not part of a specific plan but, in the head's opinion, if a teacher is genuinely enthusiastic for an artist-in-school project it is important to support them.

For the head the young female actors fulfilled an invaluable brokering role between school and community. In his view they created a bridge and dialogue between the experience and values of the school and the world of the local estate where children spend most of their daily lives.

Observations on the project from participants and others

'It gave us options, at the end of the day we have to make our own decisions ... when it's done like this it makes you want to learn about it, I thought, that girl could be me ... they didn't just say 'that's wrong' as they normally do in school when they show you a video and give you sheets of paper with questions, this was for real and it really made you think.' *Pupils, eighteen months after the play.*

'I learnt a lot about what it (drug abuse) can do to you. You've got to be your own person and not let other people make you do things. It's easy to get in a situation where you just go along with what everybody else is doing because if you don't everyone will think you're a wimp. Things from the play keep coming back to me.' *Pupil.*

'At one moment in the play there was a bit about drugs and period pains. There was blood everywhere, it was really funny and over the top. I'd heard something about drugs and period pains before but this really brought it home to me and made me think. Even the boys listened to it and they're, well a lot of them, stupid about things like that!' *Pupil.*

'PSS (Personal and Social Skills) is a space that encourages students to think for themselves, where you can express a view. A stimulus like this puts the issues into a real life context and helps a lot. The actors involved in the performance are able to do things teachers couldn't.

It is helpful that they are outsiders, with whom the pupils can readily identify, who are really putting across the same message that we ourselves are promoting. Restrictions of time for PSS teaching can lead towards a straight delivery of information and facts relating to different issues. A creative input like this is an invaluable opportunity to give depth and meaning to the programme.' *Head of PSS.*

Tensions

'We organise our PSS timetable a year ahead. We need information well in advance to discuss and plan what resources, visits and guests we can use in the PSS programme without disrupting the wider timetable, especially in the upper school. Besides releasing pupils for an event of this nature we have to release the relevant staff, otherwise we will not gain maximum benefit.' *Head of PSS.*

'I appreciate it's difficult for members of staff when another department asks for kids to be taken off the timetable. But it makes me angry when I have gone to a lot of trouble booking a performance, especially when it relates directly to the curriculum, to look round and see some of my colleagues nonchalantly marking books. I think it's offensive to the artists and a bad example to students.' *Teacher.*

'The performance needed blackout facilities for the night club scenes and unfortunately our curtains in the hall allow a lot of light through. It knocked some of the visual edge off the show for me, though it didn't detract from the audience's engagement with the action.' *Teacher.*

'The excellent follow-up material from the company and drugs unit was extensively researched and detailed; too much so, in fact, I had to create a more accessible precis that I felt my colleagues in other subject areas would have time to assimilate and use in the classroom.' *Head of Drama.*

Summary of project

'The girl that could be me' was initiated by the regionally funded TIE company working in collaboration with the county council drugs education unit. The head of drama had frequently acted as a broker between their work and a range of subject areas in school. He saw that this project related directly to work being done in drama, PSS and English.

The head of PSS recognised the relevance of the project to the PSS teaching programme. Unfortunately the tour of the production did not coincide with the timetabling of the drugs module. The publicity material for the show arrived at school some three months before the tour. The PSS timetable is planned on a yearly basis. This has implications for pupil and staff availability which in a large secondary school can be a complex issue. The difficulty illustrates the need for long-term planning and co-ordination between arts organisations and schools.

The production did have a powerful impact on the young audience and provided a stimulating focus and reference point for discussing drugs related issues. For students of the arts it was an opportunity to appraise a powerful and polished piece of live, professional theatre. According to staff and pupils the writing, direction, acting and singing was of a very high standard indeed. It was a memorable experience. This is reflected in a discussion, some eighteen months afterwards, in which pupils' recollection of detail was impressive. They could recall in detail the storyline, the rich characterisation, the lively music and the issues raised. The pupils identified with the vividly portrayed characters who illustrated a contrasting range of role models and attitudes. The pupils had learnt that they themselves are responsible for the choices they make, and observed that the production had helped them to see the consequences of making alternative, real-life decisions.

The head of PSS endorsed the response of the pupils and commented that, in order to work effectively as a PSS teaching resource, the production must first of all be effective as a piece of theatre; the message may be right, but if the theatre is weak then it will be lost. In the view of the head the show acted as a bridge between school and the local estate where most of the pupils lived.

There was no workshop process after the show and some of the pupils regretted that there was no opportunity to meet and talk further with the actors. However, the impact of the performance, still evident after a period of eighteen months, illustrated the value of a powerful piece of theatre as an effective learning resource in a range of curriculum areas, and as a rich experience in its own right.

Project seven: Don't cue the urchins

Description of project

Our journey ends with two folk musicians in the South West and a comprehensive school, with a large proportion of pupils in the lower ability range, on an outer-city estate. The estate is typical of many across the country. Built in the late sixties and seventies, it has a paucity of cultural and social amenities. The dearth of cultural activity is reflected in arts provision within the school which is widely agreed to be erratic. According to the headteacher children are 'bereft' of cultural experience and few will have had the opportunity to visit the theatre or a gallery.

The headteacher, and other community figures, have persistently lobbied the local authority to invest cultural resources in the estate. She was pleasantly surprised one day when the city arts officer rang to say that the Leisure Services Department had allocated resources to support a short residency at the school. The residency would involve a couple of well-known folk musicians, with extensive experience of working in schools, who were already familiar with the school and area. With laudable enterprise she promptly set about finding matching resources from the A4E (Arts for Everyone) Lottery scheme!

The headteacher was quite clear what she wanted. In her view the arts were not taken seriously enough in the school; a view endorsed by the OFSTED inspection some weeks earlier. What was needed was an outside input to inject 'rigour and depth' and to raise the profile of the arts in the eyes of children, teachers, parents and governors. The two musicians had the skills to make this happen. They would produce a serious piece of music theatre that would involve teachers and children researching, composing, rehearsing and performing alongside each other. The main pupil involvement would be from year 9 and above and opportunity would be given for as many people to participate as was practically possible. The A4E grant would enable them to employ a designer to complement the artists' music and drama expertise.

A series of meetings were held involving the head, deputy head, lead teacher (from the English department) and the artists to establish the nature and structure of the project. The planning stage was all too brief and nobody seemed fully happy with the text to be used as a starting point. However, as locally gathered material would be adapted alongside the text the artists agreed to go ahead. A period of scheduled visits for song-writing, devising and rehearsals during the day and over weekends culminated in a whole week in the summer term to bring the show to readiness. A formal contract between artists and school was drawn up and signed.

The aim of the artists was to get children involved 'in something with dignity' that could be linked to drama, music and the wider curriculum. The artists expressed concern regarding the choice of a historical topic about children; the production could all too easily become a 'cue the urchins' extravaganza. As artists they were also surprised that the project's direct relationship to the curriculum was given such low profile by everybody else. The text explored issues arising from a famous incident, early in the twentieth century, in which children at a village school had gone on strike in support of their teachers. The artists saw the potential of the material to relate directly to aspects of the curriculum in English, music, drama, dance, religious education, history and geography. In a school project they, as experienced community artists, view the curriculum as part of the working context with which they need to familiarise themselves.

The artists had a wide range of music and drama skills, which meant that a large number of pupils could effectively be engaged in the composition and performance of the original music, the rehearsal of set pieces of text, the devising of locally researched drama and dance material, and acting in the imaginative stage setting which used a medieval tradition of stage 'localities' and levels. The school had little experience of mounting an ambitious music theatre production and the creative design concept, which utilised the entire school hall space, presented a real challenge to cast, musicians and stage management.

The production ran for four nights and audiences were, according to the head and other observers, focused, responsive and enthusiastic. The small audience numbers on some nights was a disappointment to the participants. So much energy had gone into the creation of the show that the need for systematic marketing had not been recognised!

According to teachers, parents, governors, city council members and officers in the audience the quality of performance and commitment was high and the sense of achievement emanating from the children was, as one observer commented, 'like an electric charge that sent a shiver down my spine'. The audience visibly detected a different, more disciplined intention which had a ripple effect throughout the school. This was later reflected in enhanced relationships between children and staff and a more serious attitude towards the arts. It has encouraged a debate about how the school can upgrade the status of the arts in the curriculum and in staffing priorities.

Observations on the project from participants and others

'They (the artists) were like in between being a teacher and being one of us, you could talk to them easier.' *Pupil.*

'I would go as far as to say that, as a headteacher, I am at my happiest when we have good-quality artists working in school. There is a special atmosphere, an energy, it lifts you. Creativity is infectious.' *Head.*

'The production had a visible impact on parents and others in the audience. The respect from the audience was tangible, there was a recognition of a different intention. As a company of pupils and teachers they got over a school tradition of 'oh, dad's coming to make me laugh' by displaying an unprecedented focus and discipline. The artists 'professionalised' us. There is no doubt that the project gave the school a much more rigorous and disciplined attitude to the arts. It shows we recognise the values of the arts and we have serious intentions to develop them now in the school.' *Head*

'We were concerned at first that some of the teachers were not taking the work as seriously as ourselves and that this could have an impact on the pupils. It was important to overcome attitudes, which emanated from some staff, that school productions have a set pattern and that 'you'll get it right' by the last night. We had to work hard to embed the professional discipline that you get it right on the first night, and the second, and the …' *Artist.*

'I was really impressed with how the musicians could go and listen to elderly, local people telling stories and talking about songs they knew, and then fold it all into the show.' *Sixth former.*

'I learnt a lot about patience, about working in a team and not getting ratty with each other when there's a problem.' *Pupil.*

Tensions

'The planning seemed very hurried and to an extent we were working on the hoof. We had to overcome the kids' resistance to working on more serious material than they were used to, and an attitude, from a few staff, that 'its only a play'. *Artist.*

'We found it really hard not having a proper stage setting and not having a backstage area to go when you were not 'on'. *Pupil.*

'I didn't particularly like the content, I would have preferred something we had made up ourselves like we did last year. This was a bit too serious, it was definitely the school's choice, not ours.' *Pupil.*

'It was good that we got the A4E Lottery grant to enrich the project. It is a shame that the award is a one-off grant, with no possibility of further, follow-up resources. The project had raised expectations but, financially, it left us feeling we were back to square one.' *Head*.

Summary of project

This project was supported by a small grant, at short notice, from the city's leisure services department; the result of persistent lobbying by the head and other community leaders. The head then showed initiative in applying for a matching grant from the A4E Lottery scheme which was not confirmed until after the project had begun.

The head was single-minded in defining the intentions and parameters of the project. Given limited resources and the short notice this enabled the artists and teachers involved to maintain a clear focus. It was agreed by all those participating that planning was too hurried and decisions were being made without detailed consideration of alternatives. For example, the text chosen as a springboard for the project was seen as adequate but uninspiring. However, the planning process showed a high level of trust and co-operation between teachers and artists which was reflected in the positive outcome.

The artists brought into the school a professional attitude to the arts and this was respected by staff, pupils and, eventually, several parents. The production reached what the head described as 'a new level of seriousness in the arts.' Pupils were at first resistant to the idea of working with more serious material but responded to the encouragement and skills of the artists. The pupils' devising, composing and performing skills were extended and they learnt a great deal about 'professional' discipline and working as part of a team. The production has raised expectations as to what the school is capable of achieving.

Members of staff and pupils rehearsed and performed together under the direction of the artists and one teacher from the English department. It was agreed by both staff and pupils that this had engendered a level of collaboration and mutual respect which had since then been carried over into the classroom.

Audience numbers for the performances were disappointing for the cast. This was put down to an inadequate and underconfident marketing and promotion strategy for an event that could have had a much wider impact on the local community and estate.

The school does not currently have a strong arts teaching foundation so this valuable project was not extensively followed up within the arts, and wider, curriculum. There was no formal evaluation procedure. However, the head's intention to raise the status of the arts was acknowledged to have been successful by teachers, artists, pupils and outside observers such as city council officers and members. The project has led to the head and governors planning a longer-term strategy for the development of the arts in the school. A further residency project has been planned with the artists which will be able to benefit from the experience of the first production.

A number of features can be identified from the projects that contributed towards a successful outcome. We can summarise some of these features within the original interviewing structure.

Genesis

The support and encouragement of the head is crucial. In one of the projects the head herself was the energising force. In the others the teachers involved were able to proceed feeling that the head backed their involvement and that the project fitted into the overall school vision. Some of the schools have an arts policy which includes planning for the use of artists in the school. One head remarked that, following the impact of this and other residency projects, he would include an 'arts statement of intent' in the school development plan and budget accordingly. We saw from the projects that sometimes a good opportunity arises at short notice and without overall planning it may be difficult to find resources. The differing planning cycles between school and arts organisations also caused problems at times.

In order to promote work of the highest standards teachers need access to information and advice regarding appropriate and available artists. Outside support from adviser, inspector, RAB officer or education agency can be invaluable.

In the majority of artists-in-schools projects that we visited the project was initiated by an arts organisation.

Planning

Artists and schools need to clarify shared aims and objectives with good communication and thorough planning. In some cases there was a formal contract agreeing terms, fees and timing. This avoids the situation, as in one of the projects, in which the school was surprised to find itself with a bill of some one hundred pounds more than expected!

Planning takes time and projects seemed to work most smoothly when this was recognised in the initial stages and budgeted for accordingly. Good planning encourages a feeling that the project is organically a part of what is happening in school and helps to draw support from other staff and parents.

Careful planning enables maximum benefit to be derived from the artist-teacher partnership. In one project artist and teacher regretted that, owing to wider organisational problems, they could not practically work together during the residency. They knew they had much to learn from each other. An essential dynamic of the partnership was therefore lost.

Organisation

Schools have to invest time in organising timetabling, room changes and staff cover to prevent avoidable tensions. One of the projects involved more than one school and lack of organisational support at one end created embarrassment for the artist. Several months after another project one of the artists recalled warmly how the head's meticulous organisation of materials, space and even cups of tea, had made a huge difference to how she experienced the project; feeling welcome encouraged her to give of her best.

Preparation

Good preparation generates a sense of expectation and involvement for pupils. One of the projects was to be the initial stimulus for an ongoing programme of study. Preparation before the event here was deliberately low-key. In another project the artist requested that the students undertake an extensive research process prior to his arrival.

Engagement

The actual input from the artist is the living reality of a project. At its best such an experience may live in the memory for a lifetime. The diversity of engagement between artist and school is richly demonstrated in the projects. Engagement ranged from a 'one off' performance to a three-year programme of workshops, interviews and presentations.

Teacher and artist have to maintain trust during the engagement. One of the project teachers described how much he respected the local company's work and felt secure in their experience and skill. He also knew that his own role, as either outside spectator or participant, would be discussed and explained clearly.

Follow-up

Several teachers described how the projects had lifted their confidence and enhanced specific teaching skills. One teacher remarked on the high standard of creative writing she herself was now drawing from her class. She had also gained enough confidence to run an INSET course for colleagues. Similarly, in another project the head justified the focus on one class and teacher because the experience would have a ripple effect throughout the school.

In one project artist, children and teacher expressed disappointment that a lack of resources prevented the artist contributing directly towards ongoing progression and development. In another school the lack of a strong arts teaching foundation meant that the follow-up was unpredictable.

Evaluation

Evaluation of the projects varied between 'we did it in the pub afterwards' to a three-year evaluation with a University Institute of Education. In one instance the teacher involved was so exhausted by the end that she was unable to carry out the evaluation process she had planned.

Evaluation is important in developing practice and improving quality and the process need not consist of a mountain of yet more paperwork. In one of the projects the arts organisation involved acted as a broker and provided a clear, simple evaluation format for school and artist.

5 SUMMARY OF KEY FINDINGS

Evidence

- There is a growing body of evidence and testimony to indicate that the work of artists, in schools and colleges, enhances the quality of teaching and learning in the classroom and makes a significant contribution to the quality of school life.

- Input from artists can enhance a school's ability to meet the demands of the Inspection Schedule as outlined in the OFSTED *Framework*. The *Framework* indicates, for example, that inspectors should make judgements as to how the school promotes spiritual, moral and cultural development, the teaching of reading and writing, pupil motivation and positive attitudes to such issues as drugs, bullying and racial harmony.

- Input from artists may relate directly to aspects of the National Curriculum in a wide range of subject areas.

- There is evidence from heads, teachers, children and parents that working with artists can help to increase pupils' self-esteem and, through the encouragement of positive attitudes, enhance the learning of core literacy skills.

Provision

- There are excellent models of artists-in-schools activity throughout the country that reflect a rich diversity of practice. However, the overall picture is patchy and fragmented.

- It is self-evident that high-quality inputs from theatre, dance or music companies are expensive and rely extensively on subsidy in order to be financially accessible to schools.

- There is evidence indicating that the activities of small-scale, specialist arts education companies, such as in TIE, have declined over recent years. There has been an increase in the educational activities of ACE- and RAB-funded, mainstream arts organisations.

- The work of an individual freelance artist, such as a poet or visual artist, can more easily be accessed through local partnership arrangements with, for example, LEA, RAB and school or group of schools.

- Arts education agencies have considerable potential to broker links between school and artist. They can encourage schools to define and communicate their own artistic needs. However, overall provision is uneven.

- Artists in school do not work within a nationally agreed framework or funding strategy, and many feel isolated from information, advice and networking.

- Innovative partnership is the most effective way to promote good artists-in-schools practice. Long-term thinking and planning are essential.

Delivery

- Input from outside artists is most effective in the long term when there is already good arts teaching in the school.

- Collaborative, systematic planning and organisation between artist and school is necessary to derive maximum benefit and prevent avoidable tensions. The support of the headteacher is crucial.

- Many schools do not include the work of visiting artists in their school development plan and find it difficult to locate resources at short notice.

- Evaluation and follow-up are essential features of good practice but too often get marginalised.

Training

- Ongoing programmes of training for teachers to work with artists and for artists to work in education are necessary to maximise the benefits of the work. There are some good models of artists-in-schools training programmes throughout the country that could form the basis of a national network.

Evaluation

This review is part of a series of initiatives that endorse the values of creativity and the arts in education. The HMI Specialist Advisers in art, dance, drama and music have recently published *The Arts Inspected*, a review of good teaching in the arts (Heinemann, 1998). The RSA has launched a three-year research programme to look in depth at the effects and effectiveness of a good education in the arts. QCA is involved in major research into cultural development. The DfEE and DCMS have set up the National Advisory Committee on Creative and Cultural Education to make recommendations on the creative and cultural development of young people

The theme of partnership weaves its way through the review in various forms. The active collaboration of OFSTED with such bodies as ACE, the RSA, QCA and the new Advisory Committee could significantly enhance understanding of the value of using artists in education. For example, OFSTED's collaboration with the joint RAB and ACE initiative on evaluation would enable arts officers and inspectors to use shared criteria in the identification and affirmation of good practice. Information from OFSTED inspectors would be invaluable in enabling the Arts Council to monitor the development of arts education agencies.

Wider involvement of inspectors in the critical appraisal of projects could significantly enhance the status of the work and help to raise expectations and professional standards. Their involvement could encourage teachers, and trainee teachers, to make connections between input from artists and their own curriculum concerns and priorities. OFSTED's collaboration with ACE and the RABs could also be invaluable in the much-needed process of helping to disseminate and encourage stimulating models of practice.

OFSTED is not a funding body but has a keen interest in the identification and promotion of good practice. How a project is funded and managed is part of that practice. Identification by OFSTED inspectors of good work could provide important information for those bodies that do have specific responsibility for funding artists in education.

Artists, both within and from outside school, have a special contribution to make towards learning and the quality of school life. We look forward to OFSTED's further involvement in the development of this work and in the promotion and encouragement of the highest standards.

Annex: Artists in schools throughout Europe

In 1995 The Culture Committee of the Council for Cultural Co-operation, in Strasbourg, established an initiative which is now called 'Culture, Creativity and the Young.' A questionnaire was sent to all Culture Committee delegations seeking their co-operation in a study of arts education provision. Over twenty positive replies were received.

The survey, representing an official view of practice, confirms that there is huge variation in provision (Robinson, 1997:11). All national policy statements of education confirm the importance of cultural development and the promotion of artistic opportunities for young people. In practice the status of the arts is less secure. The arts, especially music and art, are significant in primary education after which they usually become optional. The arts feature more strongly in Northern Europe policy statements compared to the South. In all cases the arts have less status than mathematics and science.

The questionnaire included a section on the use of artists in education. Again, the responses varied hugely. For example, in Spain and Turkey there was little formal use of artists in schools. In France, Norway, Sweden, Italy, the Netherlands and the UK there is a rich diversity of practice.

Artists-in-schools programmes are funded by a range of means including Ministries of Culture and Education, Arts Councils (UK and Norway), Regional and Municipal Authorities, schools themselves and parent-teacher associations. The Netherlands Institute for Arts Education (LOKV) has a budget to 'encourage co-operation between primary schools and local government in order to improve provision for the arts and artists in education' (Robinson, 1997:107). In France pupils may go on 'culture classes', intensive periods of arts activity at an appropriate site, and the Ministries of Culture and Education encourage 'systematic co-operation' between schools and cultural institutions' (Robinson, 1997:72-3). In many instances economic constraints restrict the level of central co-ordination and financial support as, for example, in Italy – which still manages to promote many schemes at the local and regional level.

There is wide disparity between how different countries throughout Europe value the arts in education, though the general trend is that the arts are regarded as of less importance than the more traditional, academic and scientific subject areas. Ken Robinson, Director of 'Culture, Creativity and the Young', makes the following observation:

> 'Consequently, access to arts teaching is often restricted to those children who are either thought to have particular talent in these areas, or, just as commonly, to those whose parents can afford to pay for extra tuition. Despite the rhetoric, the arts are not normally seen as priorities in the long-term development of national educational systems.' (Robinson, 1997: 12).

References

Abbs, P. (1987) *Living Powers: The Arts in Education.* Falmer Press, London.

Allen, G. and Dalrymple, L. (1997) *'Forbidden Fire': An Evaluation.* University College of St Mark & St John, Plymouth.

Arts Council of England (1992) *Drama in Schools.* London.

Arts Council of England (1996) *Consultative Green Paper for Education and Training in the English funding System.* London.

Arts Council of England (1997) *Leading Through Learning.* London.

Arts in schools Project Team. *Arts 5-16: A Curricular Framework.* Oliver and Boyd, Harlow.

Atherton, S. (1991) *LMS - TIE - RIP, Dance and Drama, 10 (2),* summer, 17-20.

Braden, S. (1978) *Artists and People.* Routledge and Kegan Paul Ltd., London.

Bruner, J. (1996) *'The Will to Learn' in Towards a Theory of Instruction.* Harvard University Press.

Bryant, J. and Dust, K. (1997) *Developing an Education Policy/Strategy. Guidelines.* Southern Arts and Eastern Arts.

Clark, L. (1984) *Theatre, Memory and Learning. An Exposition of the Action and the Act of a Reflexive Evaluation.* Unpublished M.A. Applied Research in Education at East Anglia University.

Cook, J. (1997) *'Dancing with the Agencies - Who Calls the Tune?'* Unpublished manuscript. Rent a Role at the Barbican Theatre, Plymouth and The Barefoot Project, Plymouth.

Cox, M. (1997) *Article 31. Children and the Arts.* Play Train, Birmingham.

Dahl, D. (1990) *Artists' Handbooks 1. Residencies in Education.* AN Publications, Sunderland.

DFE (1995) *The National Curriculum.* HMSO, London.

Department of National Heritage (1996) *Setting the Scene. The Arts and Young People.* London.

Downing, D. (1996) *Artists in Leeds Schools.* Leeds City Council Department of Education.

Downing, D. and Jones. (1989) *Special Theatre.* Gulbenkian Foundation, London.

Elliston, K. (1994) *Evaluating the Effectiveness of Theatre in Health Education for Sexual Health Education in Schools.* Unpublished dissertation Master of Science in Health Promotion and Health Education, University of Wales.

Eastern Arts Board (1977) Draft Paper on the Evaluation Research and Development Initiative.

Harland, J. (1990) *An Evaluation of a Performing Arts Experiment in a Special School*. Educational Research Vol. 32 Number 2 Summer 1990.

Harland, J. and Kinder, K. and Hartley, K. (1995) *Arts in Their View. A study of youth participation in the arts*. National Foundation for Educational Research.

Harries, S. (1983) *Writers in Education*. London Arts Board.

Harries, S. and Shaw, P. (1994) *Arts Education Agencies*. The Arts Council of Great Britain, London.

Harries, S. and Shaw, P. (1995) *Arts Education Agencies: A Progress Report*. The Arts Council of England, London.

Hogarth, S. and Kinder, K. and Harland, J. (NFER). (1997) *Arts Organisations and their Educational Programme*. Arts Council of England, London.

Hornbrook, D. (1998) *On the subject of Drama*. Routledge, London.

Jackson, A. (1995) *Anecdotes Are No Longer Enough*. Paper delivered to Researching Drama and Theatre in Education Conference, University of Exeter.

Jackson, A. (ed.) (1993) *Learning Through Theatre. New Perspectives on Theatre in Education*. Routledge, London.

Kushner, S. (1991) *The Children's Music Book*. Calouste Gulbenkian Foundation, London.

Labour Party (1997) *Create the Future. A Strategy for Cultural Policy, Arts and the Creative Economy*. London.

Lockwood, F. (Ed.) (1997) *The Workbook: The central written resource for the ABO National Education Programme 1997*. The

Association of British Orchestras, London.

Manser, S. (1995) *Artists in Residence*. London Arts Board and St Katherine and Shadwell Trust.

Maslow, A. (1962) *Towards a Psychology of Being*. D. Van Nostrand, New York.

McDonald, I. (1980) *Professional Arts and School*. Arts Council of Great Britain, London.

Morley, D. (1991) *Under the Rainbow: Writers and Artists in Schools*. Northern Arts and Bloodaxe Books.

NAWE. (1998) *Writing in Education. Issue Number 14*. York.

NFER (1997) Newsletter re: '*A Report to the Arts Council on Orchestral Education Programmes*'.

NSEAD (1997) *Newsletter Issue 3*. Corsham, Wiltshire.

Oddie, D. (1997) *The Barefoot Actor*. The University College of St Mark & St John, Plymouth.

OFSTED (1995) *Framework for the Inspection of Schools*. London.

OFSTED (1995) *Annual Report of Her Majesty's Chief Inspector of Schools*. HMSO, London.

OFSTED (1998) *The Arts Inspected: Good Teaching in Art, Dance, Drama and Music*. Heinemann.

Oxford. Parks, M.E. (1992) '*The Art of Pedagogy: Artistic Behaviour as a Model for Teaching*', in Art Education, September.

Patterson, A. (1994) *Arts in the Curriculum*. Leicestershire County Council.

Pratley, D. and Bhydderch, G. and Stephens, J. (1993) *Musicians go to School.* London Arts Board, London.

Prentice, R. (ed.) (1995) *Teaching Art and Design.* Cassell, London.

QCA (1997) *The Promotion of Pupils' Spiritual, Moral, Social and Cultural Development.* Draft Guidance for Pilot Work. November 1997.

Renshaw, P. (1995) *'New Musician New Performer'* Music Journal. Vol. 60 No 8, London.

Renshaw, P. (1993) *The Management of Creativity in Schools, Colleges and Arts Organisations.* Gresham College, London.

Robinson, K. (1997) *Arts Education in Europe: a Survey.* Council of Europe.

Robinson, K. (1980) *Exploring Theatre and Education.* Heinemann, London.

Robinson, K. (ed.) (1982) *The Arts in Schools: Principles, Practice and Provision.* Gulbenkian Foundation, London

Rogers, R. (1998) *Developing Arts Education Agencies.* ACE, London.

Rogers, R. (1993) *Education - Looking Over the Edge: The Debate: Advisory Structures for the Arts in Education.* Arts Council of Great Britain, London.

Rogers, R. (1995) *Guaranteeing an Entitlement to the Arts in Schools.* Royal Society of Arts, London.

Rogers, R. (1997) *'The Heart of the Matter'.* The impact and implications of the Education and Research Initiative. Arts Council of England, London.

Ross, M. (1988) *The Arts in the Primary school; Reforming Teacher Education.* Falmer Press, London.

Ross, M. and Kamba, M. (1997) *The State of the Arts.* Exeter University.

RSA (1997) *The Arts Matter.* Gower, Aldershot.

SCAA (1997) *The Arts in the Curriculum.* London.

Schechner, R. (1989) *Between Theatre and Anthropology.* University of Pennsylvania.

Secondary Heads Association (1995) *Whither the Arts?* The State of the Expressive Arts in Secondary Schools.

Sharp, C. (1990) *Artists in Schools: Issues and Implications.* Educational Research 32(2), Summer, 140-143.

Sharp, C. and Dust, K. (1997) *Artists in Schools.* The National Foundation for Educational Research. Slough, Berkshire.

Shaw, P. (1996) *Mapping the Field.* Association of British Orchestras, London.

Smith, N. (ed.) *The Opera Education Pack.* Opera and Music Theatre Forum, London.

Tambling, P. (1997) *An Analysis of the Relationship between Young People and Opera within the Context of Arts Education.* Unpublished Master of Arts thesis, Leeds University.

Taylor, R. (1991) *Artists in Wigan Schools.* The Gulbenkian Foundation, London.

Taylor, R. and Andrew, G. (1993) *The Arts in the Primary school.* Falmer Press, London.

Trowsdale, J. (1997) *Evaluating the Role of Artists in the Initial Education and Training of Specialist Arts Teachers.* Unpublished thesis for the degree of MPhil, University of Warwick.

Turner, E. (1997) A Paper presented to Dance Matters Conference, Nov. 1997. *Linking the Arts with Education: Can Evaluation help to Build the Bridge?*

Turner, E. and **Stronach, I.** (1993) *Arts and Education: Perceptions of Policy, Provision and Practice.* A report prepared for The Scottish Arts Council in the Department of Education, University of Stirling, Edinburgh.

Willis, P. (1990) *Moving Culture: An enquiry into the cultural activities of young people.* Gulbenkian Foundation, London.

Acknowledgements

We would like to thank the many people who have helped us during the review process.

Claire Ackroyd, Cartwright Hall; Christine Agambar, OFSTED; Sean Aita, The Royal Theatre, Northampton; The Association for Business Sponsorship of the Arts; The Association of Professional Theatres; Gillian Baker, Artist; Josanne Balcombe, Redbridge Drama Centre; Prof Barber, DFEE Standards and Effectiveness Unit; Sue Barry, Artist; Peter Bartle, Halifax Curriculum Support Team; Ian Bennett, Swindon LEA; Norinne Betjemann, ACE Education Department; Irene Bishop, St Saviours & St Olaves School; Judith Bissell, The Theatre in Health Education Trust; Art Blackburn, Teacher; Eric Bolton, HMI retd. RSA Chair; Harry Bowles, Teacher; Andrew Breakwell, Wolsey Theatre in Education; Peter Brownjohn, Belle Vue Primary School; Jane Bryant, Southern Arts; Kate Buchannan, Trinity College of Music; Lynne Buckley, St Saviours & St Olaves School; Paul Bunyan, NIAS; Lesley Burgess, London Institute of Education; Ruth Burgess, London Workshop Company; Pat Burns, Adviser for Arts, Croydon; Tony Byrne, Portsmouth City Council; Chris Cade, Elmete School; Julia Calver, Yorkshire & Humberside Arts Board; Shirley Campbell, Northern Arts Board; Nick Capaldi, South West Arts; Andy Caplan, Lambeth Education Dept; Pete Castle, Artist; Adrian Chappell, Education Officer; Bill Chatwin, Elmete School; Gordon Clay, HMI Specialist Adviser for Dance; Community Music East Ltd; Pete Coe, Artist; Heather Conne, Artist; Raymond Cook, Lambeth Children's Theatre; James Cornford, The Paul Hamlyn Foundation; David Coslett, University of Plymouth; Philip Cox, Artist; Mike Cundy, Essex County Council; Susan Daniels, Bretton Hall College; Julian Davies, Arts Access; Leonora Davies, National Association of Music Educators; John Davies, Christian Aid; Tom Davies, University of Central England; John de la Cour, Hereford Arts Education Agency; Steve Derrick, Artist; John Dinnen, Artist; Stephen Disbrey, North East Lincolnshire Council; Peter Downes, SHA; Stephen Downey, Essex County Council; Dick Downing, Consultant; Karen Dust, Eastern Arts; Scilla Dyke, Foundation for Community Dance; Fergus Early, Artist; Penny Egar, RSA; Kevin Elliston, Health Promotion Agency; David Farmer, Tiebreak Touring Theatre; David Firmstone, University College, Chester; Will Fitzgerald, The University College of St Mark & St John; John Foster, Devon County Council; Paul Foster, University College of St Mark and St John; Anne Gallacher, West Midlands Arts Board; Tony Goode, University of Northumbria; Ken Goodge, Performing Arts Adviser, Wigan; Fiona Gore, Derby Playhouse; Tony Graham, Unicorn Theatre for Children; Wendy Greenhill, Royal Shakespeare Company; Harry & Margaret Grove, Artists; Bronwen Gwillum, South West Arts; Pepita Hannah, Birmingham City Council; John Harland, National Foundation for Educational Research; Sue Harries, RSA; Jennie Harris, Royal National Theatre; Alison Haynes, Birmingham Education Arts Forum; James Hennessy, Artist and University of Exeter; Sarah Hennessy, University of Exeter; John Hertrich, HMI Specialist Adviser for English; Martin Hinckley, London Borough of Hounslow; Hilary Hodgeson, LAB Education Officer; Sharon Hogan, Westbourne First

School; Dawn Holgate, Phoenix Dance; Vikki Holroyd, Warwickshire Artist in Schools Team; Pam Howard, Hextable School; Janet Humphrey, The Royal Theatre, Northampton; Bhajan Hunjan, Artist; Tony Jackson, University of Manchester; Hugh James, East Midlands Arts; Veronica Jobbins, The National Dance Teachers Association; Diana Johnstone, Hereford Arts Education Agency; David Johnstone, Roundabout Theatre in Education; David Jones, National Society for Education in Art & Design; Margaret Jones, Sherman Theatre; Matthew Jones, Southway School; Peter Jones, HMI Specialist Adviser for Art; Rev Peter Jones, Community Priest; Phil Jones, Greenwich Education Service; Bev Joycy, HMI; Paul Kaisemann, Leeds City Council; Kate Kelly, Islington Council; Paul Kelly, Plymouth City Council; Alan Kennedy, Plymouth College of Art and Design; Tony Knight, QCA; Nigel Leighton, Drumcroon; Jane Leyland, Marks and Spencer PLC; Anne Littlejohn, The University College of St Mark & St John; London Workshop Company; Graham Long, South West Arts; Barbara Maddox, Southway School; Sally Manser, Tower Hamlets LEA; Jon Marshall, Artist; Margaret Martin. HMI; Robin Martin, South East Arts Board; Janet Matthewman, North West Arts; Dr Pat McGovern, The University College of St Mark & St John; Gail McIntyre, West Yorks Playhouse; Pete Meakin, Derby Playhouse; David Millar, Plymouth City Council; Janet Mills, HMI Specialist Adviser for Music; Ian Mitchell, Exeter University; George Morris, Artist; Caroline Moss, Milverton Primary School; Paul Murray, Hereford & Worcester County Council; Peter Muschamp, HMI; Beverley Naidoo, Bournemouth Borough Council; Lyndsey Newton, Dudley LEA; Oily Cart Theatre Company; Lyn Paine, Dorset County Council; David Pammenter, King Alfred's College; Anice Patterson, SCAA/QCA; Robert Pearce, Christian Aid; Arthur Penn, Oxfordshire County Council; Fiona Penny, Association of British Orchestras; Nick Penny, The World of Strings; Andrew Fuskek Peters, Artist; Jonathan Petherbridge, London Bubble; Elizabeth Poulsen, Incorporated Society of Musicians; Ruth Powell Thomas, Ernesettle Infant School; Debbie Priest, Borough of Poole; Barbara Pritchard-Hiti, Artist; Sarah Pym, Plymouth Barbican Theatre; John Rainer, Chair of National Drama; Shantha Rao, Annapurna Dance; Hymn Rapstoff, Artist; Neil Rathmell, Shropshire County Council; Dr John Rea, The University College of St Mark & St John; David Read, OFSTED; Geoff Redman, Bishop Grosseteste College; Andy Reeves, Speakeasy Theatre; Prof Peter Renshaw, Guildhall School of Music & Drama; Peter Riches, Eggbuckland School; Denise Richardson, Westbourne First School; Simon Richey, The Gulbenkian Foundation; Joanna Ridout, Oily Cart; Shantha Rao, Annapurna Dance; Andy Reeves, Speakeasy Theatre Company; Biddy Roberts, Warwickshire Artist in Schools Team; Prof Ken Robinson, University of Warwick; Rick Rogers, Journalist; Jim Rose, HMI, Director of Inspection, OFSTED; Malcolm Ross, University of Exeter; Mary Scurlock, Hillingdon Education Services; Maggie Semple; Stephanie Simms, Cumbria Arts in Education; Karen Simpson, Action Transport Theatre Co; Caroline Sharp, NFER; Nona Shepherd, Artist; Kirsty Smart, Northern Artists into Schools; Eddie Smith, Wakefield LEA; Martin Paul Smith, Artist; Pauline Smith, Floating Point Science Theatre; Roger Smith, Milverton Primary School; Sheila Smith, Hextable School; Eric Spears, National Association of Headteachers; Philip Spellacy, Artist; Madge Spencer, Artist; John Stephens, Trinity College of Music; Jeff Stratton, Artist; Catherine Sutton, Royal Festival Hall; Marion Talbot, QCA; Michelle Tallack, Anglia Polytechnic University; Pauline Tambling, ACE; Jane Tarr, University of West England; Jackie Taylor, Devon Curriculum Advice; Ann Tennant,

City of Birmingham Symphony Orchestra; Chris Thompson, Artist; Hazel Townson, Artist; Fraser Trainer, London Sinfonietta; Rosemary Tromans, The University College of St Mark & St John; Jo Trowsdale, University of Warwick; Triangle Theatre; Paul & Marilyn Tucker, The Wren Trust; Eileen Turner, Sterling University; Peter Turner, Bread & Circuses; Adrian Vinken, Theatre Royal, Plymouth; Judith Waddington, Kirklees Metropolitan Council; Phil Waite, Gloucester City Council; Mary Walker, Pandora's Daughter; Tony Wells, Farnborough School; Anya Whitehead, London Borough of Camden; David Whitfield, Devon County Council; Daria Wignall, Havering Inspection & Advisory Service; Keith Willis, Surrey County Council; Malcolm Wray, Warwickshire County Council; Trevelyan Wright, Salisbury Playhouse; Sue Wyatt, The Cholmondeleys & The Featherstonehaughs.

Printed in the United Kingdom by The Stationery Office Limited

J60647 387321 C25 12/98 19585